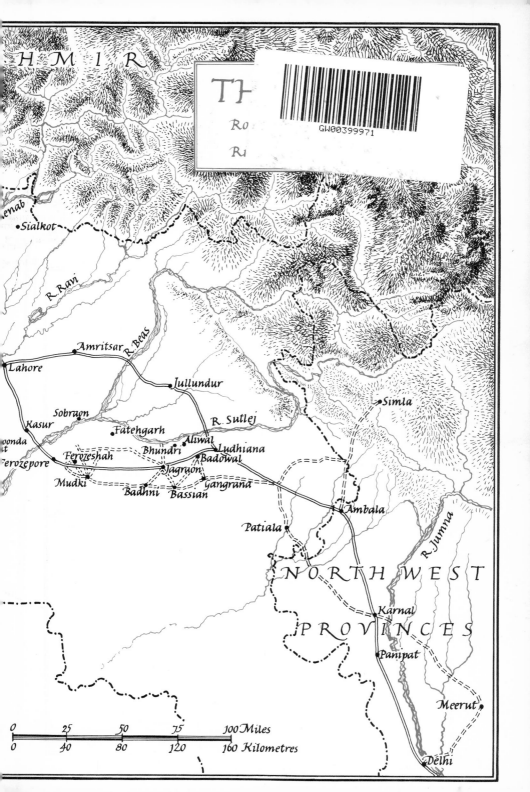

SERGEANT PEARMAN'S
MEMOIRS

by the same author

THE CAPEL LETTERS
Being the Correspondence of Lady
Caroline Capel and her daughters
with the Dowager Countess of
Uxbridge from Brussels and
Switzerland
1814–1817

ONE-LEG
The Life and Letters of
Henry William Paget, K.G.,
First Marquess of Anglesey
1768–1854

SERGEANT PEARMAN'S MEMOIRS

BEING, CHIEFLY, HIS ACCOUNT OF SERVICE
WITH THE THIRD (KING'S OWN) LIGHT DRAGOONS
IN INDIA, FROM 1845 TO 1853,
INCLUDING THE FIRST AND SECOND SIKH WARS

Edited by

THE MARQUESS OF ANGLESEY
F.S.A.

JONATHAN CAPE
THIRTY BEDFORD SQUARE
LONDON

SBN 224 61466 5

PRINTED IN GREAT BRITAIN BY
EBENEZER BAYLIS AND SON LTD,
THE TRINITY PRESS, WORCESTER, AND LONDON,
ON PAPER MADE BY JOHN DICKINSON AND CO. LTD.
BOUND BY A. W. BAIN AND CO. LTD, LONDON

CONTENTS

ILLUSTRATIONS

Illustrations

Illustrations

Rare coloured lithograph by Laby and Ogg, after C. B. Spalding; published by T. Maclean, 1849.

The picture is inscribed: ' "It is with great pleasure I embrace the opportunity of stating to you officially that your squadron, commanded and led by you, made a most brilliant charge, breaking through a large body of the enemy's elite infantry, completely disorganising and routing them" – Extract from an official letter addressed to Capt. L. Fyler, 16th Lancers, by Brigadier Macdowell, c.b., commanding 1st Brigade of Cavalry at the Battle of Aliwal, 1846.'

In the possession of the Parker Gallery

Illustrations

Illustrations

received across the shoulder, and the marks (*bottom right*) of the
spear thrust in his side (*see p. 91*)

> In the possession of the Regimental Museum of the Queen's Own Hussars,
> Warwick

John Pearman in old age

> In the possession of George Pearman, Esq.

Pearman's Punjab Campaign Medal, 1848–9

> The medal was designed by William Wyon, R.A. (1795–1851), chief
> engraver at the royal mint.
>   The obverse shows the diademed head of Queen Victoria. On the reverse
> is shown Major-general Sir Walter Gilbert receiving, in the presence of
> his troops, the surrender of the Sikhs. Their arms lie at his feet. In the
> background are hills with palm trees. Above appears: TO THE ARMY OF
> THE PUNJAB.
>
>   In the exergue appears the date: MDCCCXLIX.
>   The two clasps are for Chilianwala and Gujrat.
>   The ribbon is dark blue with yellow borders.
>
> In the possession of George Pearman, Esq.

MAPS

11

EDITOR'S NOTE

THE manuscript of these memoirs is entitled *Memos. of the late Sergeant John Pearman of H.M. Regt., 3rd or King's Own Light Dragoons.* The small vellum-covered volume in which it is contained is the property of Sergeant Pearman's grandson, Mr George Pearman. He brought its existence to my notice, allowed me to make a transcript of its contents, and did not complain when I kept the original for long periods. He also made available the photographs of his grandfather and of his campaign medals which appear facing pages 32, 64 and 129. His interest and active assistance during the preparation of this book for the press have been most encouraging. Further, he gave me much background information, which proved invaluable. For all this I am deeply grateful.

Others whose assistance I wish to acknowledge with thanks include: Mr Robin Mackworth-Young, M.V.O., the Librarian at Windsor Castle; Mr D. W. King, O.B.E., the Chief Librarian of the Ministry of Defence Library; Mr S. C. Sutton, the Librarian and Keeper of the India Office Library, and his assistant, Miss Harrold; Mr John Paris, M.A., B.LITT., the Director of the National Army Museum; the London Library; Mr Hector Bolitho; Mrs Pat Brayne (whose immaculate typing is a delight to all who employ her services); Mr F. M. Delmar; Mr Roger Fulford; Brigadier O. F. G. Hogg, C.B.E.; Mr R. G. Hollies-Smith, F.R.G.S., F.S.A. (SCOT.) of the Parker Gallery; Mr Harold James, M.C.; Mrs H. St G. Saunders of

13

Editor's Note

Writer's and Speaker's Research; Major J. S. Sutherland, M.B.E., The Queen's Own Hussars; Mr Philip Mason, C.I.E., O.B.E. (Philip Woodruff); and Lieut.-col. W. H. Unett. I am grateful, too, to Mr Denys Baker who has made clear and effective maps out of my muddled scribblings.

* * *

Sergeant Pearman's lack of a formal education is reflected in the almost total lack of punctuation, in the primitive grammar, and in the phonetic spelling which occur throughout his memoirs. To make the narrative readable, I have been obliged, regretfully, to add punctuation, to ameliorate the idiosyncratic grammar (without, I hope, destroying its flavour), and in many cases to correct the spelling.

Except where there are repetitions, very few omissions have been made from the original manuscript. This does not apply, however, to that part which I have placed in Chapter V. Here Pearman indulges in page after page of philosophical, political and social reflections, few of which are original or of particular interest. From these I have made no more than a representative selection.

I have modernized and standardized the spelling of most of the Indian proper and place names.

A.

Plas Newydd
Anglesey
February 1968

INTRODUCTION

THERE are few enough detailed accounts by rank and file members of the 'Queen's Army' in India before the 1857 Mutiny. Of those that exist most suffer from defects. Some were written with an eye to publication and too often suffer from pretentiousness. Others were polished up, rehashed or mangled by over-zealous editors. Very few have the authentic, straightforward touch, the intimacy, and above all the immediacy of Pearman's unvarnished narrative.

It was written some time after the events which it describes, but there is evidence for supposing that it was based upon letters which he wrote home at the time (see p. 145). From the point of view of military history it has some importance. While not adding a great deal to our general knowledge of the campaigns, it does supply a number of new details.

For example, among Pearman's descriptions of the actions at which he was present during the first and second Sikh Wars, there are two which throw especially interesting light upon them. The first is his account of the engagement at Badowal on January 21st, 1846 (see p. 35). This is much more detailed than any other. It shows very clearly what large risks Sir Harry Smith ran in trying to by-pass the enemy without making a wide enough circuit.

The second is his statement that when Ouvry's squadron of the 3rd Light Dragoons broke ranks and raced along the river bank at Ramnagar on November 22nd, 1848, so as to

15

make the Sikh guns reveal their number, 'some of the horses got set fast, up to the belly. The men had to leave them.' (See p. 72.) This is the first certain evidence that the existence of 'quicksands' was definitely established in the course of that exploratory gallop. It makes William Havelock's later charge with the 14th Light Dragoons over the same ground even less excusable than has hitherto been supposed.

*   *   *

The Sikh Wars were the last of the seventy or so 'small wars' of The Long Peace, as it is euphemistically called, which were fought by the British Army in almost exactly the same way as in the Peninsula. A formal 'Order of Battle' was still generally adhered to; neither uniforms nor weapons were greatly different. The last occasion on which the senior commanders had seen serious action was against Napoleon, more than three decades earlier, and four or five years before Sergeant Pearman was born.

Virtually all the generals and many of the officers commanding regiments were 'Peninsular Men'. Six years later, the Crimean War had made this title one of opprobrium, standing for everything that was out of date and wrong with the army; but in the 1840s men were still proud to be thus distinguished.

If the great reforming experience for the army at home was the Crimea, it was the Great Bengal Mutiny which shook the army of India out of its old-fashioned ways. After that traumatic experience nothing was ever the same again.

Before the Mutiny, the Honourable East India Company was still the ruler of British India, even though its powers had been gradually eroded over the years. Before the Mutiny, the 'European' regiments of the Queen's Army at home (of which Pearman's was one) were only hired out to the Company to serve as a backbone to its own army of British-officered native troops. The Governor-General was still the appointee of the Company's Directors in Leadenhall Street. After the Mutiny, all that was changed: rule was exercised by Whitehall through a Governor-General who was the direct representative of the Queen, and the Company's Indian army became the Queen's Indian Army.

The Sikh Wars, therefore, mark very clearly the tail-end of a long period of British military history: one that was dominated by techniques developed by the great Duke of Wellington. They were also the last wars to be fought without the mixed blessing of war correspondents in attendance. For this reason such accounts as Pearman's have a special significance. Without the records of eye-witnesses like him, historians too often have to rely almost exclusively upon the inevitably prejudiced dispatches of the generals.

* * *

Pearman was considerably above the ordinary run of men in the army in the mid-nineteenth century. For one thing he could read and write, whereas even as late as 1858, one-fifth of the rank and file could do neither, and another fifth could read but not write. Further, he successfully resisted the brutalization to which many succumbed, and retained a certain intrinsic sensitivity and spirit of inquiry. In India, for instance, he was 'very fond of roaming about the country and conversing with natives — a people I always find very kind,' he wrote, 'if properly treated by us, but I am compelled to say some of our men used the poor native very bad.'

In old age Pearman became excessively class-conscious. Even during his army career he evinced signs of resentment at the gap between officer and man, and the different standards which applied to each. He gives as one of the reasons why he found his time in India the most enjoyable of his career, that 'it places the great man and the poor on a footing. I have oftimes put my foot on a dead officer as we put his body under ground, and said to myself "Where is your rank now?" Then Mr Officer was not the same *tyrant* in India that he was in England.' Elsewhere he notes with approval the conduct of a young officer who always ducks his head when under fire, but who frankly explains that he cannot help it.

His views on war were not always typical of fighting men in the nineteenth century. After the battle of Chilianwala in 1849, for example, he wrote: 'The rain came down as if to cleanse us from our past sin, for I verily believe man was not made by God to kill his fellow man.' This comment is very characteristic of its writer and his views. At the time of writing it he was a month short of his thirtieth birthday. He had been in the ranks of the 3rd Light Dragoons for just over five years. During four of these he had been stationed in India. In that time he had seen action in three battles and three lesser engagements, coming unscathed through them all.

Before he left for home again in 1853, he was to see one more major action — the victory of Gujrat, which effectively finished off the second and last Sikh War. Of the crisis of that battle he wrote: 'The air became filled with shot, shell and smoke. Trumpets were sounding, drums beating, bugles sounding, colonels and other officers hollering ....' This is but one of many examples of his ability to use words to evoke the excitement of battle. Graphic as some of his descriptions are, they never forsake the realms of realism for the high-flown rhetoric of more sophisticated writers.

When it comes to the uglier side of war, the very matter-of-fact tone of Pearman's recitals serves to accentuate the horrors they illustrate. In the action at Badowal, the very first in which he took part, a corporal next to him had a leg shot off. To those near him, the poor man said: 'Comrades, take my purse!' (But Pearman, ever practical, took his gun instead, tossing away his own inferior model.) 'We had not got far,' he continues, 'when another ball struck Harry Greenbank in the head. It sounded like a band-box full of feathers flying all over us.'

Time and again he evokes for the reader the dangers and hardships which beset the common soldier a hundred and twenty years ago: the hunger, the thirst, the cold, the heat, the lack of what we today should consider absolute necessities, the universal resort to drink to make life bearable, the occasional, but entirely accepted, floggings.

He reflects, too, the feelings of soldiers throughout the ages (except, perhaps, our own) when, just before his baptism of fire, he writes: 'All our talk and hope was: "Shall we be there in time to get the *medal?*" ' And again, as a veteran, before his last battle: 'We lay on the ground, talking of home, old comrades dead, and the coming day, and who would see the sun again set.'

Of the generals he does not say much, though he approves of Sir Harry Smith, who was probably the best of them. The proverbial bravery and bluff kindness of Sir Hugh Gough, the Commander-in-Chief, were generally much admired by his men; but Pearman was more sceptical. He implies on more than one occasion that he thinks the high casualties in some of the battles resulted from Gough's impetuosity. Again, when 'the old man', as he calls him, spoke to the troops 'a lot of stuff' about 'the laurels to be gained for our country', Pearman observed, sardonically, that there was 'not a word about the pension you would get if you got cut about'.

19

Whatever he may have said and thought about the military life after, in bitterness, he had left it, Pearman shows himself fully aware of its occasional delights. He noted with pleasure, for instance, what forcibly struck every man on arrival in India, that all the menial tasks, even for the youngest recruits, were performed by myriads of 'black servants'.

In spite of a hasty temper and a touch of meanness in money matters, Pearman must have been good company, a steady and upright friend and a credit to his regiment.

*　*　*

No less absorbing than the record of his martial experiences, especially for the general reader, is his chronicle of what happened to him after he had left the army; how, as a policeman, he dealt with the criminals who crossed his path; what it was like to be inspector at Eton College in the '60s and '70s, and what befell his family when his children caught scarlet fever.

Sadly disenchanted though he became towards the end of his life, Pearman when he moralizes, and expresses his disillusionments, exhibits an interesting and very human side of a man whose capacity for thought was a rare thing in the class from which he came. The last part of his memoirs may be depressing, but it is none the less an important part of an engaging social document.

CHAPTER I

JOHN PEARMAN was born on February 24th, 1819. He came from a line of small farmers in South Oxfordshire. Little is known of his father, Robert, though at one time he seems to have been employed in the forest at Windsor, probably as a verderer. He was born at Nettlebed, Oxfordshire, and married a Miss Elizabeth Woodham who was Welsh, and is said to have been governess to the children of Mrs Jordan by the Duke of Clarence, later King William IV. Robert is buried at Kingston-on-Thames, and Elizabeth at Ealing. She was born in 1778 and died, aged 87, in 1865. The dates of birth and death of her husband are not known.

John, who was possibly the eldest of their children, started work as a sawyer, 'at the age of thirteen years and nine months'. In 1840, when he was twenty-one, he thought it

time to give up such hard work, which brought little more than a living to myself, but much for my employers. The railway started,ᵃ and I was employed as a guard, and remained at it for two years; but not liking London, I was far from being settled, although we made good wages and were not worked too hard. But I felt I should like to travel and see other countries.

Well, one day I had a tiff with the superintendent, and my

ᵃ The Great Western Railway. Brunel's great line extended at this time only as far as Swindon.

21

temper being very hasty, we nearly got to blows. So I made up my mind to be a soldier.

He was twenty-four when he

enlisted at the Essex Serpent public house, Charles Street, Westminster, on August 26th, 1843. I was sent to the depot at Maidstone, in Kent, for drill and instruction, the regiment being in Bengal in the East Indies.

Pearman's regiment was the 3rd Light Dragoons,[a] which has a long and distinguished history. Its first great action was the battle of Dettingen in 1743 against the French in the War of the Austrian Succession. In that battle the 3rd, only two squadrons strong, after lengthy exposure to artillery fire, charged nine squadrons of the flower of the French cavalry, not once, but three times. Three-quarters of their men and horses and all but two of their officers were killed or wounded.

In the Peninsular War the 3rd's great moment came at the battle of Salamanca. It was one of three regiments in Le Marchant's brigade. The other two were the 4th Dragoons and the 5th Dragoon Guards. Wellington,

[a] Formed as 'The Queen Consort's Regiment of Dragoons' in 1685, the regiment became known in 1688 as 'Colonel Leveson's Dragoons'. It was renamed 'The 3rd Regiment of Dragoons: The King's Own Regiment of Dragoons' in 1714, and in 1818 'The 3rd King's Own Light Dragoons'. On the reorganization of the army in 1861, it became 'The 3rd King's Own Hussars', and in 1921 'The Third The King's Own Hussars'. In 1958 it was amalgamated with the 7th Hussars in 'The Queen's Own Hussars'. The 3rd and the 4th Hussars are the two senior hussar regiments in the army.

The regiment's battle honours are: Dettingen (1743), Salamanca (1812), Vitoria (1813), Toulouse (1814), Peninsula, 'Cabool 1842', Mudki, Ferozeshah (1845), Sobraon (1846), Punjab, Chilianwala, Gujrat (1849), 'South Africa 1902'; 27 in World War I and ten in World War II.

The regiment bears on its appointments the White Horse of Hanover on a red field within the Garter. Its motto is *Nec Aspera Terrent*. This is usually translated either as 'Difficulties do not deter us', or 'No hardships deter us', or, more simply, 'Undaunted'. When the White Horse of Hanover is used as a badge, the ground beneath its feet is shown as very rough. This, it is said, is to justify yet another translation of the motto: 'Rough going does not deter us.'

when he saw that Marmont by over-extending his left had given him his great chance, personally ordered Le Marchant, who was advancing between and behind two infantry divisions, to charge at the first opportunity. He chose a moment of confusion when, though some of the French battalions were breaking, the leading British infantry brigade, confronted still by large numbers, thought itself lost. With a ghastly roar, never forgotten by the survivors of the onslaught, the 4th and 5th, supported by the 3rd, all in perfect order, emerged from the smoke, thundering past the astonished British infantry. The brigade broke into the flank of the first two battalions, who vainly tried to form square to meet it. Some were sabred, others left for the infantry to pick up. Next, the second French line, three complete battalions, in better order than the first two, had to face the relentless sabre-work of the British horsemen. These, too, after firing a volley which emptied numerous saddles, were rent asunder, their component parts scattered. Almost without altering pace, hastily dressing their line and closing the gaps, the three regiments, by now intermingled but still under control, were led by Le Marchant against a further three battalions. These, much blown from doubling for over a mile to get into position, only had time to form imperfect squares before firing a volley at their assailants. They fired too late, for though many of the leading dragoons fell, the impetus of their horses could not be stopped. There followed a deadly fight of sabre against bayonet which ended for the French in total flight. Le Marchant was killed outright; only exhaustion stopped his men. Wellington, when he saw the initial charge exclaimed: 'I never saw anything so beautiful in my life.'

Since 1840, all the regiments of Light Dragoons (3rd, 4th, 13th and 14th) had been clothed in blue uniforms. In the 3rd the lapels, collars and cuffs of the jacket, or 'coatee', were faced with scarlet. It was double-breasted with two rows of buttons, eight in each row. Gold bullion pieces were worn at the back of the waist, and the small skirt was closely pleated. The officers' lace was gold, and so were the cap lines (the distinguishing mark of an officer), and the crimson-striped girdles. The trousers had two stripes of gold lace for 'dress' and two of scarlet for 'undress'. The head-dress was a shako, almost cylindrical in shape. Made of black beaver, it was bound round the top by gold lace. The plate at its front was of a cross pattern, with the regimental device below a crown. From the shako sprouted a large drooping plume. For the officers this was made of swan's feathers. In India horsehair was substituted, and the shako was covered with a white quilted cover either with or without an anti-sun curtain (see illustration facing p. 49). Full-dress coatee and overalls were the usual campaign kit. The horse furniture included a round-ended shabracque on which were crowns and the regimental title abbreviated. Over the saddle was a black sheepskin.

In the year of Queen Victoria's accession the 3rd left for its tour of duty in India. Its numbers were increased to the normal Indian establishment of eight service Troops with one recruiting or depot Troop left at Maidstone. The eight service Troops consisted of 44 officers and 702 rank and file. Under Sir Joseph Thackwell the regiment took part in the first Afghan War, a squadron under Captain Unett (see p. 91) distinguishing itself in the action of Tezin on September 13th, 1842.

When the regiment returned to England in 1853, only 47 of the 420 rank and file who had sailed in 1837 were still with it.

CHAPTER II

On June 4th, 1845, Pearman was one of a draft of sixty men which embarked for India from Gravesend in the *Thetis*.[a] There were also sixty men for the 9th Lancers, forty for the 80th Foot and four for the 39th Foot, as well as thirteen women and thirty-seven children.

Four young married women of the 3rd Light Dragoons were smuggled on board and taken out with us without leave.[b] It was a very fine day and many people accompanied us, both friends and sweethearts; so time passed merrily on the road [from Maidstone to Gravesend], the band of the Depot playing. We arrived at Gravesend about midday, and were soon embarked—the bands playing 'Fare thee well, love, now thou art going over the wild and trackless sea. Smooth be the wave and swift wind blowing, though 'tis to bear thee far from me.' When all were on board the good ship, the word was given to weigh anchor, and then the band played 'God Save the Queen'. We were now employed in getting out our sea kits and utensils for cooking, and being told off into messes—six each mess. Then we got our hammocks down and were shown how to tie them up and get into them. We were as close together as the fingers on our hands.

Four days later they

[a] Possibly the Hon. East India Company's sailing brig-of-war of that name.

[b] Only a limited number of women was allowed to accompany troops going overseas. Wives had to draw lots to determine which should go with their husbands and which stay. The existence of these four wives when they arrived in India would have been totally unrecognized, and no official provision would have been made for them.

lost sight of land, and most of the men were very sea sick, but in a few days more most of us were becoming *sailors*. There was little to do on board ship but play cards and sing in fine weather: parade twice a day, once for health, clean feet and body, and once for muster. Food was very good and I got very stout. A comrade named Hamilton, a tailor, learnt me the use of the needle, which I found afterwards to be very useful to me. On our passage we caught several porpoises and we ate some of the flesh. I did not much care for it. We caught also several sharks, and inside of one we found a steel tobacco box, a pipe, part of a straw hat and part of a man's shoe. We had two plays when the ship lay becalmed. I played in both. In *Macbeth* I took Banquo.

After passing Tenerife, no more land was seen till the Bay of Bengal was reached.

About 5 o'clock on the afternoon of October 3rd, 1845, our ship cast anchor in front of Fort William at Calcutta. The Garrison Major came on board, and said we were as fine a lot of young lads as he wished to see (but little did we think that ere four months had passed, one-third of our sixty lads would be no more, but such was the case). That night we lay in front of Fort William. I cannot forget that night. We were nearly mad with the heat between decks and the mosquitoes; no man ever can forget. The next morning at 5 a.m. we were put on a steam boat and taken up to Chinsura where we were landed after 120 days on board. Our things were carried to the cantonments by the black servants, and as soon as we got into our rooms there was a very nice breakfast for us, consisting of beef steaks, soup and many other things which we did good justice to, after being so long on salt food.

We had a parade at 10 a.m., got white clothing served out, took our sea clearance money, and like soldiers, went off at once to spend it. At night we could not sleep, what with the heat and the noise the jackals made. In the morning before it was light the black men came into the rooms, which are very large open rooms, only iron and wood rails for walls. They sat at the foot of your bedstead, with a large earthen vessel on their heads, holding two or three gallons, calling out 'Hot coffee, sahib'. This was done so much that my comrade, by name Makepiece, but wrongly named, threw a boot at the poor fellow, broke the vessel, and the hot coffee ran down his body, but did not scald him. Of course Makepiece had to pay for the coffee.

At this place there was in my time no want of grog and the men were half tipsy all day. The canteen was open all days, with a sentry to see no liquor was taken away, but you could buy 16 drams or 3 pints one dram, for one rupee or two shillings, and this arrack or rum was over-proof.

October 5th William West of ours was taken with cholera and died in a few hours, and one of the 80th Foot, his wife and baby, all died in twelve hours, of cholera. There were about 2,000 recruits and a few invalids in the barracks, and the deaths from all causes amounted to two or three every twenty-four hours. Those that died in the day we buried at sundown, and those that died in the night we buried at 5 a.m. We soon got used to it. Taking things altogether we enjoyed ourselves at Chinsura.

On October 20th, Pearman's draft, amongst others, was embarked on two boats and towed by steamer

first to Calcutta, then down the Ganges, and then into the Sunderbans or 'the Floating Islands'. At night the boats anchored in mid-river for fear of wild beasts. There were plenty to hear at night and a great number of alligators of all sizes from a yard long to four yards, and as large round as a small horse in body. They only lay in the water or on the bank. I never knew anyone touched by them myself. Our officers shot at many of them.

Poor Martin McGee was taken with cholera and died the 2nd day. We buried him near a mosque on the bank in a gutteree, or cotton quilt. His wife grieved very much. They were both Irish but nice people. She married again, one Thomas Fleming at the regiment.

We were packed in these open flat-bottomed boats like pigs in a pen — men, women and children with not room to walk, and at night we nearly lay one on the other. The women and children at one end of the boat, the soldiers at the other — a lasting disgrace to England. The blacks could pity us. In this way we went up to Allahabad, a distance of nearly 600 miles. The food we got was bad, sometimes salt rations. The men grumbled; in fact nearly mutinied, and then it was made better.

We saw many strange sights on the river Ganges: the dead bodies floating down, and large birds eating the flesh as they went along. Some times our boats got aground and that caused much delay. At length we had no more wood or coal to get upstream, and men were sent on shore to press men to pull the boats up. We called at many places: Monghyr, Dinapore, and Benares, and other places, but the country had become of a very sameness, and we cared but little about anything. Most of our time was taken up playing cards. Sometimes we were allowed for an hour on the bank to stretch our legs and we made the most of it. On our arrival at Allahabad, we were taken into tents, about a mile from the fort and remained several days, and roamed about with nothing to do and got very happy. We forgot all our ill usage on board the boats. I don't think soldiers bear malice. I was in a tent with Sergeant-major Baker. A tent in India holds sixteen men, four in each corner, with the arms in the middle.

We commenced our march. The fourth day from Allahabad we had three men flogged, one hundred strokes each: drunk on rearguard.

At Cawnpore the drafts were inspected by

Major-general Sir Joseph Thackwell [see p. 138], who gave us great praise for our conduct and general appearance. A great deal of sickness was in the station. We lost Sergeant Robinson from fever, and his wife from cholera, and Jack Hawkins was left back when we marched. He died with bowel complaint. About four days after leaving Cawnpore, we came to an encampment where were the 53rd Foot[a] (which regiment had marched one day in advance of us). They had a man die, and had buried him in a *tope* [grove] of mango trees, but the jackals had taken the trouble to get him up and pick his bones. His head was off his body, and the flesh eaten off. The skull and jaws were together and covered with blood. The women had just arrived in camp and got out of their hackeries [bullock carts], when a man of our regiment named H. J. Potter took up the head and ran after the women with it and very much alarmed them. They did scrawl [*sic*] out! Potter was stopped three days' grog for his pains.

We had a parade at 5 o'clock p.m. under the trees, when sad to say the men fell down on parade as fast as they could be carried to the hospital tent. Some seventeen or eighteen had to be taken in. It was a jungle fever that attacked us. On the road, as they were carried in the dhoolies, or stretchers with a cover over, the blood ran from their mouths and noses. About thirty sick were now being carried in dhoolies by black men. Every day Mrs Barnes, on their arrival in camp, got

[a] The 53rd was founded in 1755. In 1782, it became 'The 53rd (Shropshire) Regiment of Foot'. Since 1920 it has been 'The King's Shropshire Light Infantry'.

water and washed the blood and dust from the poor fellows' mouths and got oranges for them. We had to take our turns to wait on them. Poor Joe Blake died first and we buried him on the side of the road. I was lance-corporal and read the funeral service over him.

At Lucknow, Pearman heard for the first time that

the troops on the front stations were taking a campaign against the Sikhs, a warlike race, standing some of them much over 6 feet high, some 6 feet 6 inches.

The Sikhs were originally a reformed Hindu sect, living in the Punjab ('the land of the five rivers'). Founded in the fifteenth century, this purely religious community had gradually adopted a military organization in addition to its devotional discipline. The famous Khalsa, the Praetorian guard of the Punjab, was instituted at the end of the seventeenth century.

War between British India and the Sikhs became virtually inevitable when their great ruler, Ranjit Singh, died in 1839. It was he who had made the Khalsa into a formidable, disciplined army. At his death he possessed 'the only army in India capable of meeting the Company's forces on equal terms'.[1] It was he who had brought together the various Sikh confederacies into a coherent state. It was he who had extended his domains to the west, to the north and to the south. Only to the east did he make no conquests, recognizing that the power of Britain was bound to overwhelm him if it were challenged. He had most scrupulously observed his treaty obligations at all times.

His death was followed by a ferocious struggle for power. This, unhappily, was even more protracted than was usual in an oriental, medieval-type state. Assassinations and riots followed each other in quick succession, but no ruler emerged from the chaos strong enough to subordinate the army to his will. In September 1845, the elected regimental committee (*panchayat*) of Lahore, the capital of the Punjab, took over the reins of government.

The court, nominally headed by a small boy who was reputedly Ranjit's son, supported that part of the army which favoured war with the British. It saw that it could not 'stand another month against the army ... and that the vengeance of a foreign army', to quote Sir Henry Lawrence, who knew the facts as well as anyone, 'would be a lesser evil than the fury of its own.' It was decided, therefore, 'to fling the soldiery upon British India, supplying them with every possible means of success, taking, if unsuccessful, the chance of clemency and forgiveness, and, if victorious, the merit and profit of repelling the English from Hindoostan.'[2]

As the crisis mounted, British troops had been moved nearer the frontier. At the end of 1844, a pontoon train was brought forward to the river Sutlej, in case a move on Lahore became necessary. By the opening of hostilities, some 40,000 men and over 90 guns were assembled between Meerut and the frontier.

The Sikhs, with an army of some 50,000 men and 100 guns, crossed the Sutlej on December 11th, 1845, and war was inevitable. Part of this army advanced to a position near Ferozeshah. Another part threatened but did not attack the isolated garrison at Ferozepur,[a] which numbered no more than 7,000 men. Its nearest supports were 5,000 men eighty miles away. Another 10,000

[a] It was fortunate for the British that no attack was made. It would have been easy for the Sikhs to march to Bassian, the main British depot in the area, and to capture that, before any considerable force could have been brought against them. There is evidence that treachery on the part of the Sikh leaders was responsible for this missed opportunity. Soon after the Sikh army had marched, Lal Singh, one of its two commanders, sent a messenger to Captain Nicholson, the agent at Ferozepur, giving him details of the Sikh intentions and expressing the hope that they would remain good friends. (Extracts from John Nicholson's journal, L 2/Bk 169, Punjab Government Records; cited in Mahajan, J., *The Annexation of the Punjab*, 1949, 30.)

were 160 miles away. These had been ordered to move up three days before the Sikh invasion started. At Meerut, 275 miles from the Sutlej, were a further 9,000 men.

All these troops were now formed into 'the Army of the Sutlej', and hurried forward. A respectable part of them, including the 3rd Light Dragoons, which Pearman was on his way to join, arrived at Mudki on December 18th. So did the Governor-General, Sir Henry Hardinge, and the Commander-in-Chief, Sir Hugh Gough. (See pp. 134 and 135.)

There followed the first battle of the war. It was the battle of Mudki, nicknamed 'midnight Moodkhee', since it continued well into the darkness. The Sikhs were defeated, but at considerable cost. The 3rd Light Dragoons alone lost 61 men out of 497. Their splendid and dashing charge against batteries placed at the edge of a jungle caused the Sikhs to dub them 'the Devil's Children', since they came upon them 'like a flash of lightning'. They also acquired the sobriquet of 'Moodkhee Wallahs'.

Three days later the two-day battle of Ferozeshah was fought. It has been described by a good authority as one of the most momentous 'and certainly the hardest fought-out'[3] of the battles engaged in by the British in India. The Sikhs lost 73 guns. The number of their killed alone has been put at between 2,000 and 3,000. The British casualties were 2,877, of which 720 were killed. The 3rd Light Dragoons again distinguished themselves. Their loss in men was 148, and in horses 197. In the two battles of Mudki and Ferozeshah they had lost only nine short of half the number of men with which they had arrived at Mudki. Fortescue rightly claims that 'few regiments of horse in the world can show a finer record of hardihood and endurance'.[4]

*　　*　　*

Sergeant John Pearman,
3rd Light Dragoons,
c. 1854

Since the photographers of
those days graded their fees
according to the sitter's rank,
Pearman borrowed a trooper's
tunic, thus obtaining his portrait
at the lowest rate. He then
painted in his sergeant's
chevrons with gold paint

Below: Two troopers of
the 3rd Light Dragoons
grooming picketed horses
in India, 1846

Sikh cavalryman of the 1840s

Pearman's party now made its way to Delhi

to be served out with arms and ammunition. We had twelve stand of old arms with us—the old Brown Bess,[a] with flint locks (these were for our guard). Strange as it may appear, the twelve old stand were retained by the men, although there were hundreds of thousands of stands of arms in the arsenal. The gun I had was deficient of a cock to hold the flint; the gun of Private Goodwin had no screws to hold on the lock; the gun of Private Roberts had no ramrod, and several others were like them. With such arms we were taken into action.

The women and children were left behind at Karnal, and the various drafts

moved on to the front without any encumbrance. We now commenced the march in right earnest, sometimes twice a day, and all our talk and hope was: 'Shall we be there in time to get the *medal*?' About the fourth day from Karnal we had a second march at 8 at night. About 10 p.m. I was on the advance guard with six men. We were about a quarter of a mile behind the rear guard of the 53rd, when suddenly that regiment sounded 'Form Square', which they did. The rear guard of about twenty men remained out, and formed by themselves. We, being recruits, did not know what to do. I fell my six men in, under a tree. It was very dark. Our detachment formed a square, when some few of the enemy's men (cavalry) rode round us and left us, neither party doing anything. We ended our march that night at 12 midnight,

[a] The 'Brown Bess' flintlock smoothbore musket was, during most of the 18th and the early 19th centuries, the regulation infantry weapon, until the introduction of the rifle made it obsolete. The 'Brown' derived from the colour of its wooden stock. The 'Bess' was either a corruption of the 'buss' (i.e. box) in 'blunderbuss', or a humorous feminine equivalent of the 'Brown Bill', the name given to the halberd with which the British infantry was formerly armed.

pitched our tents at once in front of a mud fort, by name Bassian. Next morning after breakfast we went out to drill, and while at drill an orderly rode in. It sounded 'Dismiss', and then 'Strike Tents', and in half an hour we were again on the march. No one seemed to know where—no road—over sand and through jungle. Anyway, at about 4 o'clock in the afternoon we could see a large camp, and soon found out it was our own army, under the command of Sir Harry Smith. [See p. 137.]

After the battles of Mudki and Ferozeshah, the Sikhs, though defeated, had not been demoralized. Their army recrossed the Sutlej at Sobraon. There they awaited reinforcements. So did the British. On January 6th, the troops from Meerut began to arrive at Gough's camp. Among these were the 9th and 16th Lancers.[a] The Sikhs now once again crossed the Sutlej, and took up a strong position opposite Sobraon. At the same time, sixty miles to the east, a smaller force crossed near Ludhiana. Its object was either to intercept Gough's siege-train which was lumbering laboriously towards Bassian, or more likely, merely to plunder Ludhiana and its environs. To deal with this threat, Gough detached Sir Harry Smith, with half of his infantry Division, some cavalry (including the 16th Lancers, but not the 3rd Light Dragoons) and artillery. It was with this force that Pearman's party of drafts now made contact.

One of the 16th Lancers came as our guide into the camp.

[a] The 9th was founded in 1715, and known by its Colonels' names till 1751, when it became 'The 9th Dragoons'. In 1783 its name was changed to 'The 9th Light Dragoons'.

The 16th was founded in 1759 as 'The 16th Light Dragoons'.

Both regiments together with the 12th and 23rd Light Dragoons were converted into Lancers in 1816. Both regiments saw service in the Peninsular War, the 16th gaining six battle honours, but the 9th only one. The 16th, but not the 9th, was present at Waterloo. The 9th arrived in India in 1842 and left in 1858; the 16th in 1823 and left in 1846.

Badowal, January 21st, 1846

At 5 o'clock we got our tents and put them up. We made some tea, had a wash and went down to the 16th Lancers to see whom I knew; but at 8 o'clock we were ordered to our own tents to hear General Orders read. These were that the whole camp would get the next day's rations, and march at 12 midnight in one column, and move on to the cantonments at Ludhiana.

We got on the march at 1 o'clock a.m. It was very dark and cold for India. We marched all the morning, with only one halt of about half an hour. At about 10 a.m. on January 21st, 1846, I was looking at our Left Front, when I saw something glisten in the sun's rays. I said: 'Sergeant-major Baker, there is the enemy.' He replied: 'You be damned!' He had been very drunk just before we marched. He had been down to old mates in the 16th Lancers. He had hardly replied when: 'Bang! bang!', and two balls whizzed over our heads. A third ball went into a regiment of sepoys [regular native infantrymen], and knocked over three or four men. The 53rd was taking ground to the left, when a ball passed through them, striking the ground in front of us, close to me, and bounded over our heads.

At this time we were not loaded, but Major Mythyus, in command, gave the order to load, but several of us could not, as our guns were no use. We now got an order to move to the front, and at that moment a ball came and knocked down five. A corporal of the 80th Regiment had his leg knocked off. He said: 'Comrades, take my purse!' I took his gun and tossed my own away. We stepped over them, and passed on, but had not got far, when another ball struck Harry Greenbank in the head. It sounded like a band-box full of feathers flying all over us. He was my front-rank man, and his brains nearly covered me. I had to scrape it off my face, and out of my eyes, and Taf Roberts, my left-hand man, was nearly as bad.

35

Our guns now commenced to fire on the enemy. We still continued the march, sometimes towards the enemy, and at other times towards Ludhiana, men falling every few minutes. No man of the 53rd Regiment, or our own detachment, can ever forget that day: forced marching for some days previous, and marching that day from one a.m. until 5 in the evening over thirty miles and under an Indian sun, with Brown Bess, 120 rounds of Ball Cartridge, and coat at our backs. We had nothing to drink on the road. Some of the men's tongues were protruding from their mouths. At last the men could go no farther, the enemy cavalry following close on our rear to cut up the stragglers. Sergeant-major Baker became beat, and lay down. I said: 'For God's sake, George, think of your wife and children.' He had two children. He looked at me, and said: 'I can't.' A private named Robson, a fine young man, lay down with him.

We moved on a little. When the cavalry was about to charge us, we were ordered to form square, but were unable to do so. We made one corner, but got confused. Roberts said to me: 'Jack, be steady. We will have one each.' And we both up with our guns. I had not suffered so much from thirst as some men. Roberts made water in his cap and drank it. Just as we became so confused, the 16th Lancers came down at a trot in open column of Troops, and wheeled into line between us and the enemy, and saved us. If they hadn't, none of our detachment would be here to tell the tale. They trotted towards the enemy's cavalry, but they would not stand for the Lancers. They retired.

The 53rd were at this time nearly all fallen down, but began to rally, and so did we, but not until many of our 200 had fallen down and been killed: Ted Mouse, Henry Hazard and many more — I forget their names. At last we got in sight of Ludhiana, three or four miles off, when Sir Harry Smith came to us, and looked at us with tears in his eyes. He said: 'Poor boys, lay down now and rest for a time.' Sir Harry shot the two guides himself. They were to have taken us wide of the enemy to Ludhiana, but they took us into the range of the enemy's guns.[a]

Where we lay down, there was a large shallow pond, and into this we all went to drink. There were horses, camels, elephants, men, bullocks all at once. The water was nearly like treacle, but down it went. While this was going on many of the 16th Lancers were fetching in men of the 53rd, and our detachment, on their horses in front of them.[b] By this means they saved many men that, had they not done so, must have been killed. The enemy took all our baggage, and the stores of all the hospitals, killed all our sick and the wounded on the field, and took about twenty prisoners, one of them being Doctor Banyon of the 62nd Foot, who had fallen out from our detachment to see to the wounded men.

One of the men of our Regiment, named Cumber, was taken prisoner. He was stripped naked for their sport, and when naked and being hunted about for sport, he managed to run from them. They fired several times at him, he said. But they missed him. He came to Ludhiana about 10 at night naked. He found his way by following the noise on our march.

That day my meat — (I got a piece of meat in the night) — was about half cooked, and was the round bone of the shoulder with a piece of meat attached. This I had in my haversack. I sucked this, and that was what stopped my

---

[a] This sounds like rumour. Certainly there is no mention in Sir Harry's account of the action of treacherous guides. Nor is the incident mentioned in any other account.

[b] 'Some of our poor infantry', wrote a corporal of the 16th Lancers, 'were so exhausted that we were obliged to carry them ... on our horses.' (Letter of Corporal F. B. Cowan (n.d.): Graham, Col. H., *History of the Sixteenth, the Queen's Light Dragoons (Lancers) 1759 to 1912*, 1912, 112.) The 53rd Foot remembered this with gratitude for many years. So did Pearman's detachment.

thirst. When I saw the others so bad I passed it along the ranks, each having a suck. It was soon gone. This was all we had that day.

Thus ended Pearman's first taste of action—the so-called battle of Badowal. It had come about when Sir Harry Smith discovered the enemy, to the number of 8,000 men with 40 guns, encamped at that place. Since he had but 4,000 men and 18 guns of his own, he tried to by-pass the Sikhs to the south, so as to effect his original intention of joining up with the garrison at Ludhiana. This he managed to do that evening, though losing 200 men, including many sick and wounded, and nearly all his baggage, in the process.

Next morning we called the roll. There were 17 of my regiment's recruits missing, 14 of whom had been killed. Out of our detachment of 200, 47 were missing; 31 were found to be killed, and 16 made prisoners by a man who had charge of the enemy's guns: a deserter from the East India Company's troops in 1836. He had risen to the rank of General of Artillery. This deserter saved the 16 men's lives as prisoners.

Sir Harry Smith came and looked at us on parade on the 22nd, and told us there were no rations to be got. Each man would get two rupees, and do the best he could with them. I and two others went into the town to try and buy something to eat, but we could not get anything. The natives had got nothing and all the men in camp wanted. I got a ram's head with the wool on. This we took to camp and when we got back we had a pound of elephant's cakes given to each man. I soon eat my lot. One of the men got an earthen pot as large as a pail. This we made use of. We made a fire, put water into the pot, and put it on the fire. We then scorched the wool off the head and washed it, and put it into the earthen pot to cook. It had stewed about two and a half hours, when we heard a great stir in camp and we received orders to strike tents and march. All was now on the stir in quick time. A man named Williams tried to take out the head, when he broke the pot and the broth ran to the ground. He got the thanks of the boys. We then pulled the head to pieces, and the lucky man got a piece. It was so hot, it burnt your mouth, but we got it down and worked at the tents at the same time. We had become used to roughing it. It sounded 'Fall In', so we bundled the tent on to the elephant and ran to the parade ground to fall in, told off, and were on the way again at four miles an hour, quick march.

We now heard the enemy had changed their camp, and we were going to take up their ground, which we did about dusk. The enemy had gone eight or ten miles on to Aliwal. We were now at Badowal, where the battle was fought on the 21st.

> Here Smith concentrated his augmented force. He now had with him more than 10,000 men and 30 guns, of which 22 were horse artillery. Brig.-gen. Cureton (see p. 133) commanded his two cavalry brigades, which numbered 3,000 sabres. There were also three European and eight native infantry regiments. Two of these were battalions of the famous Gurkhas from Nepal, who, except for the siege of Bhurtpore twenty years earlier, had not before seen action under the British.
> Some of the men with Pearman now

got tents at night and some lay on the open ground. We got three tents for our men, so we were well off. The next morning I began to look out for something to eat, drew my bayonet, and went about the camp. I got some coffee from a sepoy and stole two pieces of meat about the size of an egg each. These I put on the embers of an old fire to cook. But before they were done, a young officer came to me and said: 'Where did you get them, Pearman?' I replied: 'With my bayonet, to be sure.' He sat down by the embers and looked at the meat roasting on the embers. They were nearly done, when he snatched one piece. I took the other, and we both eat it. I gave him a little of my coffee, and then went to look for more to eat. I saw many more doing the same. The young officer above-named belonged to our regiment. He had to rough it the same as the rest. He after all was very cheerful and a good fellow. He became Captain and exchanged into the Scots Greys as Paymaster when they were in the Crimea. His name was Colt.

Many of the men killed on the 21st were found and buried, and some of the men were found dead in the village of Badowal, where they had been plundered and no doubt killed, as they were naked. We found some of the men's things, and the hospital stores of the 16th Lancers broken up and destroyed. This made the men very angry—and it soon spread at last. Some of the men of the Artillery set fire to some of the houses, which were soon on the ground. In fact we destroyed the place.

On the afternoon of the 23rd a man of ours named Peter Locket—a character—came into camp. He had been left on the ground, dead drunk, when we marched at midnight on January 20th from Jagraon to Badowal, and this was the first we had seen of him. Major Mythyus tried him by a Drumhead Court Martial. He was sentenced to one hundred lashes, which he got that night, and he was put into the 16th Lancer hospital tent.

Those who could ride well were to be taken to Colonel Alexander's Troop of Horse Artillery,[a] to do duty, as the

---

[a] This was the 3rd Troop of the 2nd Brigade of Bengal Horse Artillery, commanded by Brevet Lieutenant-colonel James Alexander (see p. 133). It was one of four Bengal

Troop had lost many men and was short of them. On the morning of January 28th, between 5 & 6 o'clock, Adjutant Smyth, called 'Little Jacky' Smyth [see p. 138], of the 16th Lancers, took us through the camp in the dark. All was confusion, with camels and men and regiments getting together. At last we found Colonel Alexander's Bengal Troop of Horse Artillery, when Adjutant Smyth hollered out to Alexander — (he stammered in his speech) — 'Here,' he said, 'take these young devils, for I am Adjutant, Quartermaster-general and everything else this morning. Goodbye, Colonel'; and away he went. Colonel Alexander said, 'Can these boys ride?' Sergeant Darling replied: 'All of them.' The Colonel then said to Sergeant Douglas of the Artillery: 'Mount them, and let's get on the road.' We were soon on the horses' backs and trotted to the front alongside the 16th Lancers, who threw out skirmishers to the front.

This was the opening of the battle of Aliwal, in which Sir Harry Smith, learning that the Sikh force, reinforced by 4,000 regular infantry,[a] was about to move towards

Troops in Sir Harry Smith's force. At Aliwal it was working in conjunction with the left-hand cavalry brigade.

Lightly equipped horse-drawn guns, with their crews mounted like cavalry troopers, were first used by Frederick the Great. By reason of their speed, these were able to follow the movements of the cavalry, keep the enemy's guns and infantry at a distance, and help to pave the way for the cavalry charge. This innovation, more than any other in the age of gunpowder, made it possible for cavalry to survive in the face of increasingly effective fire power. Shortly after their introduction into the Prussian army, batteries of horse artillery, or 'galloper guns', as they were first called, were attached to cavalry formations in all the armies of Europe.

Native horse artillery was first added to the Bengal army in 1817. The 'galloper guns' which till then had been attached to each of the native cavalry regiments, were formed into three troops of horse artillery. By the time of the first Sikh War there were three brigades in the Bengal Horse Artillery, with a total of six European and three native troops. Alexander's was one of the European troops. In 1861, in the reorganization which followed the Mutiny, it was absorbed into the Royal Artillery as 'L' Battery, 'B' Brigade, Royal Horse Artillery.

[a] These reinforcements were some of the finest troops in the Sikh army. They had been trained by General Avitabile, an Italian mercenary employed for many years by Ranjit Singh.

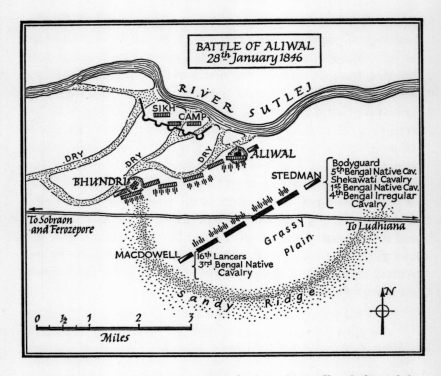

BATTLE OF ALIWAL
28th January 1846

RIVER SUTLEJ

SIKH CAMP

DRY   DRY   DRY

ALIWAL

BHUNDRI

STEDMAN

Bodyguard
5th Bengal Native Cav.
Shekawati Cavalry
1st Bengal Native Cav.
4th Bengal Irregular
Cavalry

To Sobraon
and Ferozepore

Grassy Plain

To Ludhiana

MACDOWELL   16th Lancers
3rd Bengal Native
Cavalry

Sandy Ridge

N

0   ½   1   2   3

Miles

Jagraon or Ludhiana, attacked and totally defeated it.
The enemy numbered something like 18,000 men, with
nearly 70 guns, while Smith commanded some 10 or
12,000 men, with 32 guns. The Sikh foot-soldiers occupied a curved line of shallow entrenchments, with artillery in front of them. Their right rested on the village of
Bhundri, and their left on the village of Aliwal. Behind
them was the Sutlej. This, of course, was the weakness
of an otherwise sound position.

We marched in three contiguous columns in battle array.
Our gun no. 2 in front, followed by two more, and two
behind them, and then the spare horses ridden by the black
syces or horse-keepers. About half past eight in the morning

we came in sight of the enemy. We came to a halt, and the infantry and foot artillery began to get into a line, spreading out like a lady's fan. It was a beautiful plain for miles. The sun was bright and clear.

> The plain was of hard grass-land, in contrast with the sandy desert from which the army had just emerged. It was perfect for the manœuvring of all arms, especially cavalry, and formed a semi-circular apron in front of the Sikh position.

There was the enemy in our front, three or four miles long. Our army came into line as steady as a field day. I sat on my horse and looked at the two armies. It was a lovely sight. It sounded 'Advance', and on we moved. I could see the skirmishers of the 16th Lancers were firing their carbines, and at 10 minutes to 10 a.m. the first shot, about a 9-pounder, passed over our heads. It sounded 'Skirmishers In' and back they came at a trot. On we went covered by the 16th Lancers.

At about 700 yards from the enemy, the Colonel shouted: 'Action! Front! Unlimber and prepare for action! Nos. 1 & 2 to the right; 3 & 4 to the front; 5 & 6 to the left.' We all dismounted and held the horses, when 'bang' went our guns. About the third shot I saw was making holes in the ranks in front of us. We remained more than half an hour in this way when we limbered up, mounted our horses, and with the 16th Lancers and the 3rd Native Cavalry, took ground to the left, more than a mile past the 53rd Foot [which was in the left-hand infantry brigade], near to a *nullah* or deep water-course.

At this time the firing was terrific, and looking back, the plain was covered with wounded and dead men, and horses and pieces of broken guns. Just at the time we were going to dismount, a shot struck my horse, and down he went with me.

I was not hurt. We were in a cross fire from the enemy's guns and we had seven horses down at once in my gun (no. 5), out of the eight horses. We had lost several men and they were getting short, and so were the horses. A ball struck Private Steele of ours in the head, and down he went. Our man who rode next to the gun had both legs cut off with a ball through the horse.

We limbered up again and I and Jack Reeves rode on ammunition boxes, when a shot came and struck the wheel close to me, smashed it, and the spoke struck Reeves in the thigh, but did not hurt him much. It all missed me. We had to put on a spare wheel and on we went again with fresh horses from the rear, brought up by the black syces or horselers [*sic*]. We now galloped close to the enemy, about three hundred yards, and 'Bang! Bang!' went our guns to a good tune and they did something to think about.

While this was progressing on the extreme left of the line, Sir Harry had been employing his two right-hand infantry brigades against the Sikh left. After severe fighting, he took the village of Aliwal.

The enemy commander, seeing that his left was about to be turned, brought forward his cavalry to try to re-establish it. Part of Stedman's cavalry brigade, which was on the extreme right, charged and drove it back. This was the first of at least eight separate charges made by the cavalry in the battle.

Further pressure at last forced the Sikhs to throw back their left, whereupon they tried to re-form their line at right-angles to the river, pivoting upon the village of Bhundri. To cover this movement, the enemy commander again pushed forward his cavalry. Against these Smith at once sent one squadron of the 3rd Bengal Native Cavalry, supported by another of the 16th Lancers, under Captain Bere. The native regiment, it is said, wavered; but not so the 16th, which charged in fine style.

At this time I looked to our left and saw the 16th Lancers coming on at a trot, then a gallop. I took off my cap and hollered out: 'The first charge of British Lancers!'[a] The enemy formed square, but the 16th Lancers went right on it and broke it. Such cutting and stabbing I never saw before or since.

There were, in fact, a number of distinct charges made by the two wings of the Lancers. They lost 141 men, more than a quarter of the total casualties of the army. The regiment's achievement, no less than its loss, is by any standards remarkable. The fire of the disciplined Sikh infantry, wrote Lieutenant-colonel Maude in 1903, was 'in the opinion of survivors of the Peninsula and Waterloo ... both better delivered and better aimed than that of the Napoleonic infantry'.[5] The breaking of the squares in the battle of Aliwal ranks with Le Marchant's larger-scale feat at Salamanca in 1812, and with Bock's smashing of the perfectly formed square at Garcia Hernandez in the same year.

When the exhausted survivors paraded next day, it was seen that the red-and-white pennants of their lances were so coated with dry blood that they appeared to have been starched. From that day onwards it became the regimental custom to crimp all the 16th's pennants, in memory of the battle. The tradition is still preserved

---

[a] Pearman is not quite correct in calling the regiment's charges at Aliwal 'the first of British Lancers'. In fact, the siege of Bhurtpore in 1825–6 was the first occasion, for over two hundred years, on which the lance was used in action by a British regiment. The regiment there employed was again the 16th. It is true, nevertheless, that no serious charge was made either at Bhurtpore or in the other Indian campaigns in which the regiment took part before 1846.

The 9th, 12th, 16th and 23rd Light Dragoons had been turned into Lancers in 1816. Before that the last time British Lancers were in action was at the battle of Dunbar in 1650.

in three which flutter at the present time outside the regimental headquarters.

The commander of the cavalry at Aliwal was Brig.-gen. Cureton. To him Sir Harry and others gave the chief credit for the successful use of the mounted arm, not only in the battle, but also during the tricky manœuvring before the army was concentrated, especially at Badowal.

I ran and picked up a man named Wise, shot in the leg, and put him on our gun carriage. I then ran and picked up Sergeant Stearger, shot in the neck, and put him on the gun carriage with Wise. These two men belonged to the 16th Lancers. Then we opened fire again at the broken ranks with grape and canister shot, which made great havoc.

Their army now seemed to be in full retreat towards the river, where there was a shallow ford which took them to the fortress of Valore. But before they could get over the ford we had taken all their guns — 67. One that was nearly over the river, in the ford, our No. 2 gun fired a shot at and knocked off its limber into the water. That made 68 guns. There were 5 guns taken by us, and the one in the water made 6 for the Troop. They were very fine guns, inlaid with brass on the limbers and wheels. The guns themselves were chased. Two were sent to Calcutta Museum, two to Windsor Castle, and one was made a present to Prince Waldemar of Prussia who, at the time, was making a tour of India with his staff. He joined Lord Gough's army, and was present at one or two battles.[a]

This ended the Battle of Aliwal.

[a] Prince Frederick William Waldemar (1817–49); nephew of King Frederick William III of Prussia. His sister was the mother of the mad King Ludwig II of Bavaria.

During his Indian tour he assumed the name of Count Ravensburg. The officers who accompanied him included Counts Greuben and Oriola. They were present at Mudki, Ferozeshah and Sobraon. They were with Hardinge at Ferozeshah. In his

Beside the loss of their guns, the Sikhs also lost a vast quantity of stores of all kinds. They admitted to 3,000 casualties. The British lost 589, of which 245 were from the cavalry.

Sir Harry described the battle as 'a little sweeping second edition of Salamanca—a stand-up gentlemanlike battle, a mixing of all arms and laying-on, carrying everything before us by weight of attack and combination, all hands at work from one end of the field to the other.'[6]

As a result of the victory, the British communications were secured, and the safe arrival of the siege-train was assured. Further, the enemy was at once compelled to evacuate all his bridgeheads south of the Sutlej, with the exception of his main one at Sobraon.

We retired back to where they had camped, and there found all the articles that had been stolen from the officers' bungalows at Lhudiana before they set them on fire. I took off my dirty things and put on clean ones from a Camel Trunk belonging to the 56[?]th Foot. I also found a dozen bottles of brandy, but Colonel Alexander made me break them. We picked up the wounded and then got an old Sikh tent and put it up. We got our food and grog and had a sleep and felt alright. In the evening the black servant brought me the late Sergeant-major Baker's pony. When me and Harry Proud of the 16th Lancers went into the enemy's old camp to see what we could make, I rode the pony, and Proud walked. We had been at it about half an hour, and had loaded the pony with silk gutteree and other things. I held them down on the pony

dispatch he draws attention to their conduct. 'These Prussian officers nobly sustained the reputation of their countrymen. The prince's surgeon was struck to the ground by a ball. I saw His Royal Highness instantly spring from his horse to his assistance. The prince's humanity was unavailing: death had already closed the surgeon's career.' (Hardinge to Gough, Dec. 22nd, 1845, *Despatches of Lords Hardinge and Gough, and Sir H. Smith,* 1846, 51.)

in front of me. I saw a Sikh soldier crawling towards Proud, when I called out: 'Look, Harry!', who turned round and gave him a blow on the head. He lay very quiet after that. We then went down to our old Sikh tent where some of the 16th Lancers were, and gave them some of the things, and some we parted with for grog. I tied the pony up and put the saddle under my head and lay down on one of the silk gutteree, a luxury at those times. I was soon asleep and when I awoke in the morning the pony was gone. Some of the bright boys had been about before me and sold it, and were spending the money. I gave the saddle away.

About midday I was very nearly shot. A private named Goodwin and me took a walk and were looking at the field and the dead. I had just cut off the hair and part of the scalp of a dead Sikh to make a Black Plume, and was looking at a very large dead man, near 7 feet high, and large with it, when someone fired a shot from the town of Aliwal, which struck the ground about a foot from me. So we made off to camp again and got our dinner. We had a standing camp for three or four days, and then we moved again up the country, marching sometimes right and sometimes left.

At last we got orders to join the main army at Sobraon under command of Sir Hugh Gough. The camp was a very large camp. It lay in almost a line in echelon of regiments and was twenty-seven miles in length — about 43,000 men.[a] The 9th Queen's Lancers were at the right. The distance between was filled up with infantry and artillery and cavalry, native and European. The enemy lay on the banks of the Sutlej river in an entranched camp with about 120 guns and 70,000[a] fighting men. We arrived in camp with the 16th Lancers, as we got our food with that regiment, but still rode the horses of Colonel Alexander's Troop of Bengal Horse Artillery.

[a] These figures are somewhat exaggerated.

Types of the Sikh army, 1840s.

(*a*) Officer

(*b*) Sentry

(*c*) Drummer and soldier with sword and musket

(*a*)

(*b*)

(*c*)

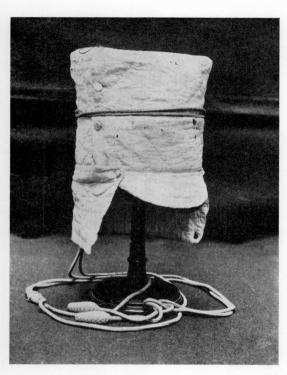

Left: Shako, with white quilted cover, as worn by the 3rd Light Dragoons on service in India in the 1840s (*see p.* 24)

Below left: Officer's shako, 3rd Light Dragoons, 1846–57 (*see p.* 24)
Below, right: Men of the 3rd Light Dragoons in India, 1845

At about 3 o'clock in the afternoon of February 9th, 1846, Acting Regimental Sergeant-major Johnson came to take us to our regiment, and several men came with him. We took a parting glass with the 16th Lancers and Artillery men, and marched for our own regiment [the 3rd Light Dragoons], about thirteen miles more. We got there about 8 o'clock at night, were seen by Lieutenant-colonel White [see p. 139] then in command of the regiment, told off to our Troops and taken to them by the sergeant-majors, who told us off to horses, as far as the horses would go, for the regiment was short of horses, so many being lost in the previous battles of Mudki and Ferozeshah. The men of the regiment behaved well to us. They had got all that lay in their power to make us comfortable, and we had a very nice supper, the officers sending us things from their mess tent. We were called and christened from that night, 'the Draft of the Bayonet Battery', on account of our marching with guns and bayonet with the 53rd, and being engaged with that weapon at the Battle of Badowal on January 21st. If any of the Draft got into trouble for years after, our Adjutant, John Sullivan, would say: 'Colonel, this is one of the Bayonet Battery.' The Colonel would then say: 'Ah, poor boy!', and let them off, saying: 'Don't you come here again, or else I shall punish you very severely, mind.' But many is the time I have heard him say the same words to the Draft. The Colonel never forgot us.

At the regiment, as we were in our tents talking to the men, about 12 midnight (for, having so much to tell them of England, and so many questions asked, we had not been to sleep although so very tired), Sergeant-major Kelly came down to the Troop and gave the order that the men would mount in the morning before day light, and make no noise. The recruits who joined on the 9th and had got horses would go with the regiment. Those without horses would remain on guard in camp and take charge of the things. I had a horse and went with the regiment.

We got on our horses and marched down towards the enemy camp at about 5 o'clock in the morning of February 10th, 1846. The long 32-pounders[a] were already down and in position, and the Rocket Platform was fixed. The guns and rockets pointed to the enemy camp. We could hear our army on the move in the dark, each regiment and the guns getting into their proper places, as told off the night before in the Divisions.

At twenty minutes after 6 o'clock a.m., our long 32-pounder guns sent several shots into the enemy's camp, and several rockets. The enemy's camp at this time had not made a move and did not know we were so close down to them. Our guns ceased fire and we waited until they got out of their tents and to their guns in their entrenchments, for theirs was an entrenched camp.

The battle of Sobraon, of which this was the opening, developed into what Sir Harry Smith called 'a brutal bulldog fight': a duel first of artillery against artillery and then of infantry against infantry. Though Gough had at his disposal ten regiments of cavalry, commanded by Sir Joseph Thackwell, there was little scope for their use. Cureton's brigade, consisting of the 16th Lancers and two native regiments, was not present. It had been detached some miles to the east to create a diversion.

[a] There were, in fact, no 'long 32-pounders' in the army of the Sutlej. Pearman probably mistook the 18-pounders, of which there was a battery at Sobraon, for 32-pounders. This is an error which even an artillery expert could easily have committed at 25 to 50 yards' distance, since the length of each piece was much the same. The 32-pounder, more often used for coastal defence than in the field, was 9 feet 7 inches long, whereas the 18-pounder was 9 feet in length.

The artillery brought into the field at Sobraon consisted of a battery of 24-pounder rockets, fired off tripods; a battery of 18-pounder guns; a mortar battery; a battery of 12-pounder 'reamers'; four 24-pounder howitzers, and two 9-pounder guns. (I am indebted for this information to Major-general B. P. Hughes, c.b., c.b.e., and Major R. St G. G. Bartelot, of the Royal Artillery Institution.)

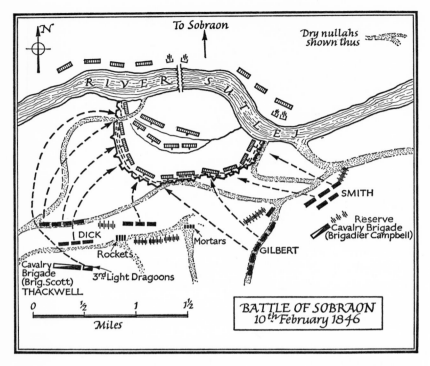

The 9th Lancers and three or four native regiments were in reserve and not called upon to take part.

The enemy bridgehead south of Sobraon was formidable, but not uniformly so. The Sikh commanders had failed to give as much attention to the fortifications as less half-hearted men would have done. Their right was especially weak, being manned by newly raised troops. The position consisted of a semi-circle of entrenchments, defended by 67 guns, and something between 20,000 and 30,000 men. A single pontoon bridge connected it with the far shore of the Sutlej on which were the reserves, including virtually all the cavalry.

Gough was faced by the necessity of a frontal attack. He had about 15,000 men and between 60 and 70 guns

with which to make it. His plan was for the heavy ordnance to smash the entrenchments, and thus prepare the
way for the infantry assaults. General Stubbs, the historian of the Bengal Artillery, says that 'the fire of our
heavy batteries, well directed as it was, did not enfilade,
and at 1,300 yards could not do much more than search
the interior of the position, when it should have been
mainly instrumental in clearing it. The siege-train, too,
had only just arrived, and the amount of ammunition
prepared on the 9th [February] was hardly sufficient.
Consequently, when Sir R. Dick's [see p. 134] [infan-
try] division was ordered forward, the fire of these
batteries had begun to slacken just when they should
have been most effective.'[7]

Our 32-pounders took the Sikhs somewhat by surprise:
such a fearful amount of bugling and tom-tomming and drum-
ming instantly succeeded. They soon returned the fire from
the numerous batteries in their entrenchments. After a few
shots to try the range, their practice became really admirable.
One of our men, Dick Neve of 'C' troop, had his horse shot,
and was ordered to the camp. The regiment was in close
column of troops. We must have been at the time from 1,000
to 1,200 yards from the enemy, according to the position of
our batteries which were all on the right or left opposite to
their left or right. But a very short time had elapsed when
their round shot shells and shrapnels came as fast as possible
to our own batteries, and amongst the troops then drawn up
pretty well out of range of the long bounds.

We had in the regiment a half-breed greyhound, and the
poor thing kept running after the spent balls until the poor
bitch could run no more, but she was not hurt. Still their shot
came among our infantry, killing and wounding a few. Such
a cannonade and noise as was now taking place, no thunder

was ever equal to. Excitement it was truly. Our batteries were firing at a most rapid rate, into the very heart of the entrenchments, hitting the bridge of boats, and even to the other side of the river, for most of our artillery and field batteries had advanced to an easy range. The firing appeared like practice in Woolwich marshes.

From 7 a.m. until about 12 noon, this firing was maintained, the round shot bounding playfully and spitefully over the plain. At about 10 a.m. all the troops for the attack had been collected in their brigades, and the brigades were united in their several divisions. The order was now given to advance, and General Gilbert's [see p. 134] Division [in the centre] threw out skirmishers to attack[?] the enemy from the right and left. The whole was now moving slowly to the entrenchments, so as to enter them by an assault, as soon as General Dick [on the left] and Smith [on the right] had gained an entrance. I saw Abercrombie's sappers making a lodgement on the works, but not before the 50th Foot and 62nd and 80th and 10th Regiments of H. Majesty had been once turned back from the batteries and again taken up the charge.

Oh, what a sight to sit on your horse and look at these brave fellows as they tried several times to get into the enemy's camp; and at last they did, but oh, what a loss of human life. God only knows who will have to answer for it. After this the infantry got some cover until the Sikhs had been driven out from the entrenchments. The 1st European Bengal Regiment[a] did good service, and a regiment of

a The Honourable East India Company's Bengal (European) Regiment was formed by Clive in 1756. In 1840 it became the H.E.I.C. 1st Bengal Fusiliers. After the Mutiny its name was changed to the 101st Foot (Royal Bengal Fusiliers), and it was brought home to Britain in 1868. A 2nd battalion was formed in 1839. In 1881 both battalions became the Royal Munster Fusiliers. The regiment was disbanded in 1922. The 1st's reputation stands very high in the history of British India. Its battle honours include Plassey, Bhurtpore, Afghanistan, Ferozeshah and Sobraon. The 2nd battalion served with distinction at Chilianwala and Gujrat in the second Sikh War (see p. 93).

Gurkhas with them—a brave mountain race. Our regiment, the 3rd Light Dragoons being in the centre [in fact, to the left of centre], we could see a great deal of the field. Such a tearing and rending of the atmosphere has never been heard before in this country.

After we had gained a lodgement, the firing slackened a little, and ours did likewise, and now comes the time of strife. Orders came for all the regiments — (regiments had been lying down for a long time) — to stand to arms. General Gilbert now threw out his Light Infantry, the whole about a hundred yards to the front, to make the demonstration of attack, while on the right and left the whole of General Dick's and General Smith's Divisions moved to the front. The horse artillery of Dick's Division cantered to the front some few hundred yards and poured in a tremendous discharge of grape. The infantry coming up in line opened a musketry fire when within an easy distance, and Sir Harry Smith's the same. Oh, what a thunder!

General Gilbert's Division was now advancing from the centre, which was taken up by the other division, and forward the long line of infantry went, two deep, for several miles in length. The enemy's shot now came on amongst the men, and it seemed difficult to fill up the gaps made; but on they go: British troops are not to be deterred. But no one could expect to escape such a fire. The enemy was now pouring in their grape at point blank range. Our artillery closed up to quarter distance, followed by the 3rd Light Dragoons, my regiment.

The advance of the army was now changed from line to echelon, and now the troops advanced. It was about 11 o'clock a.m. General Dick's Division had reached the entrenchments and was fighting like mad. A rush was made forward by the 1st regiment of Europeans with a shout, the Gurkhas close with them. The Gurkhas are dressed in dark green. They kept time and pace with our English regiments. The Sikhs were fighting bravely for their guns and camp, and our men meant to have them, and have them they did. But, oh, to tell the loss! The 1st Bengal Europeans had but 167 men on parade next morning — the remains of a noble regiment.

The Sikhs now began to retreat, but gave us parting shots as they left the parapets of the entrenchments. The Colours of two English regiments were now planted on the batteries. The enemy now formed themselves in strong close battalions to make good their retreat to the bridge of boats across the river Sutlej behind their camp. It was now our turn. It was given: 'Forward, 3rd King's Own Light Dragoons', an order the Colonel used when he was in a good temper. On we went by the dead and dying, and partly over the poor fellows, and up the parapet our horses scrambled. One of the Sikh artillery men struck at me with his sponge staff but missed me, hitting my horse on the hindquarters, which made the horse bend down. I cut a round cut at him and felt my sword strike him but could not say where, there was such a smoke on. I went with the rest through the camp at their battalions which we broke up.

Pearman is here describing the sole occasion during the battle on which the cavalry was employed. Thackwell himself led two squadrons of the 3rd Light Dragoons, followed by the 4th and 5th Bengal Native Cavalry, in single file into the enemy's position within sixty yards of its extreme right. He had found, for this purpose, one of the 'dams' left by the defenders 'at intervals across the ditch for their own convenience.... It was a miracle we were not properly riddled,' wrote Thackwell, 'but ... the guns had so sunk in the sand that the gunners could not depress the muzzles sufficiently, and therefore most of the grape went over our heads.'

Once over the parapet, the squadrons were formed, one after another, within the entrenchments. A number of charges followed, which much facilitated the entry of the infantry. Some years later, Sir Harry Smith remembered Thackwell 'shoving in your unwinged shoulder [he had lost his left arm at Waterloo] into the gap at Sobraon—the most gallant "go" of you and the 3rd Dragoons I ever witnessed.'[8]

Our regiment at this time was not 300 strong out of 700 that took the field on December 12th, 1845, and this was February 10th, 1846. In this charge we lost twenty-three men,[a] four of them out of my tent, but two of them, it was their own fault: Jack Marshall who had been *drinking* for several days. I was *told* he went out after the fighting was nearly over to attack a Sikh on horseback. His comrade, Bill Driver, a fine young man, six feet high, seeing that he was likely to get the worse of it (as we all could see), trotted out to his assistance. Just as he got to Marshall, who was just killed, a shot came and struck poor Bill. He threw up his arms, and down he came, his horse coming back to the regiment, when we caught it.

The enemy was now rushing to the ford, as the bridge was broken and on fire, and being choked up with a mass of soldiers, camels and horses with some artillery and carriages. Some of the boats [pontoons] got loose, the river being rapid at the time. The whole mass was turned into the river. From what we were told it was believed that about 10,000 souls perished in ten minutes or a quarter of an hour. Sir Harry Smith's Division came up by the river bank and killed thousands of the enemy while they endeavoured to cross the

[a] The actual losses of the 3rd were: 5 men killed, 5 officers and 22 rank and file wounded. The 3rd's total losses in the first Sikh War were 289 men and 364 horses.

river. We now possessed the entrenchments and camp, taking all their guns, nearly one hundred in all.[a] The dead Sikh bodies that lay at their guns and at the parapets! They certainly were a brave enemy, and I must say that their retreat from the camp to the river was as steady as could be, although we charged and the artillery raked them wherever they were able, to say nothing of our infantry with shot and bayonet. There were heaps of dead beside those who were drowned in the river. These were all their regular or Aeen Battalions. None of our army crossed to the other side of the river — we had done enough. The Battle of Sobraon, the most severely contested of any one in the campaign, was over and our victory complete, but had the 9th Lancers and their Cavalry Brigade been on the other side, not a man of the 70,000 would have been left.

When the Duke of Wellington heard of this battle he was Commander-in-Chief of England. He said it was a second Waterloo and ordered the Tower guns to fire a salute, which they did at 12 midnight, awaking half London. He ordered a medal with the ribbon colours Waterloo reversed,[b] which we all got. We also got twelve months' *batta* and prize money, £7 12s. 6d.

I cannot recollect the exact loss on our side, but I think the number was 5,000 killed and wounded.[c] Most of the army returned to camp about 3 in the afternoon, as our camp was left standing. We soon got into our tents. The bobagees [native male cooks] brought us our dinner, and it sounded 'Grog', so we made a good meal, had a wash, and then lay down for a sleep, and in a very few minutes all that were

[a] In fact, 67 pieces of ordnance were captured.
[b] Pearman means that the colours on the ribbon of the Waterloo medal were reversed on the Aliwal medal ribbon. The Waterloo medal ribbon is red with a blue border, while the Aliwal medal ribbon is blue with a red border.
[c] The actual loss was 320 killed and 2,063 wounded.

not for any duty were fast asleep, forgetting all about the past.

On the morning of February 11th a party was sent out to bury the dead. I remained in camp, but I heard the men say it was a dreadful sight. The farriers were sent out to shoot what horses remained alive with wounds on the battle field, for, poor brutes, they suffer much. One of our horses had one of his hind hooves knocked off, and the poor brute kept galloping about a long time. At last one of the men left the ranks and shot him.

On the morning of the 12th, we commenced the march at 5 a.m. and got to Khoonda Ghat about 3 o'clock. We crossed the bridge of boats over the Sutlej river with the artillery into the Punjab, the first regiment of our gallant army to enter the enemy's nation. We marched as far as two miles into it. On the morning of the 13th, with all the army across, we marched to Kasur, about ten miles. We found the fortress evacuated, so we took possession. Here we had a standing camp for some days, with plenty of duty on guard. As soon as you came off guard, you had to reconnoitre the country. That done, you were told off for the out-lying picquet, when you would be half the day and night on horse back, on vedette or patrolling. As soon as you had come from this you were for in-lying picquet — not to take off anything, only the bit out of the horse's mouth and hang it on the saddle which was on the horse.

On the 14th our camp was visited by the Maharajah Gulab Singh [of Jammu and Kashmir], Dewan Dina Nath, Fakir Nur-ud-din, Bhzee Ram Singh [of Jodhpur?] and 10 or 12 others, on very large elephants with splendid trappings — nearly all gold, and their dress was splendid. Some little understanding was come to, as all the prisoners taken on the 21st January at Badowal were sent into our camp, and each man was given some rupees by the order of the Maharajah. The men were glad to get back again. They did not say they had been ill-used in any way.

On February 16th we left for Lahore which city we reached on the afternoon of the 17th, and pitched our army round the city for several miles on the plains of Meen Meer, the Sikhs' old drill ground. On February 18th [the actual date was March 9th] our regiment, the 3rd Light Dragoons, was ordered on guard of honour dismounted in the great durbar tent, for the signing of the thirteen articles of the Treaty. In the tent were Sir Henry Hardinge, Sir Hugh Gough and the staff officers, and about two hundred of us with drawn swords. The Sikh chiefs also had their guard of honour. It was a grand sight. The ceremony took two and a half hours, and then Sir Henry Hardinge, the Governor-General of India, ordered the durbar to be broken up. At the same time he took possession of the young Maharajah, twelve years old, named Dalip Singh, for safety and to be sent to England. [This did not, in fact, happen till after the second Sikh War.] After this was over, our duty became much lighter as the campaign was over, and part of the army was marching back to their quarters.

The first Sikh War had been effectively finished by the battle of Sobraon. The Khalsa was humbled and its famous artillery (220 guns in all) had been captured. The Sikh state was prostrate. By the Treaty of Lahore, at the signing of which on March 9th Pearman was present, the army was limited to 12,000 cavalry and 20,000 infantry. Certain areas were ceded to the British, an indemnity of £500,000 was exacted and a British Resident established at Lahore. This solution, as will be seen, was far from final. In the event, outright annexation would have saved much trouble, blood and money;

but, at the time, the difficulties and the expense were thought to be too great.

My regiment commenced the march back early on March 22nd. The sun was now getting very hot, and before we reached our station the hot winds began to blow. We arrived at Ambala on April 7th, 1846, and took up the barracks which at that time were not finished. There had been about 700 women and children in the barracks for safety, belonging to different regiments, and a great number of officers' ladies had taken up the officers' quarters, but these were being sent back to their own regiments. The 53rd Foot was also at Ambala, and the 3rd Company, 4th Battalion of Foot Artillery, and two Troops of European Horse Artillery. The rest were black troops: 1st Native Cavalry, 71st and 64th Infantry. In all we were 7,000 strong.

We now began to get the place into order. The boxes of the men who had been killed were taken out of store, and the kits in them sold by auction by a sergeant. There were a lot in my Troop. I bought 6 dozen of shirts. A man's kit in India in quarters is 6 pairs of white trowsers, 6 pairs of draws, 3 flannels, 6 shirts, 4 white jackets, 4 puggerees, 6 pairs socks, 1 pair *setteren*[a] trowsers; for watering order: 2 pairs blue clothern overalls, one blue stable jacket, 1 dress coat, 1 shako, one cloak, 2 pairs of boots. Besides these we had many fancy things, not regimentals. The dead men's things were sold for a mere nothing, as men did not want them. We had fourteen or fifteen widows in the regiment, and most of them were married in a month after our return to quarters. Soon forgot the one dead! Some of them had had three or four husbands. One that was married made her sixth husband. She married Sergeant Gooderson of H Troop.

---

[a] Possibly *satara*, meaning a ribbed woollen cloth.

In May we got our *batta* money— £7 12s. 6d. each, and most of us had money we had made in the campaign: *Lute* [*sic*]. I sent £5 home to my friends, and it was near twelve months before they got it of Messrs Cox & Greenwood, of Craig Court, Army Agents. But they did get it.

There was a great deal of drinking, and men dying every day from the effects of drink, although we were charged 1 rupee, 12 annas per bottle of Bass Stout or Burton Ale, [that is] 3s. 6d.; but only one anna per dram, nearly a quartern, which was 3 pints, one dram, for 2s. of strong rum, and you could have as much as you liked to drink—carry none away to barracks.

We had a woman named Paddy Burns, called 'the old tin kettle'. She had a Tin Baby made with a wax face. This she would take into the canteen at evening and mimick a cry, and then give it a little grog. The child's body held more than a gallon. She would get the men to get many rupees' worth for her, and she used to then fill the child. When full she would mimick the cry and say 'Ah, I must take the young devil to its mother, I suppose', and out she would go by the sentry. This she would sell at 4 annas per dram in the night—when it only cost her one anna. When men had been drinking in the day, they would pay any amount for it in the night. Her and her husband saved a lot of money. He got his discharge, came to England, and took a Public house near London, when he failed, and afterwards we were told he went to Australia to work hard. When the child trick was discovered, she was taken before the Colonel (White), with the baby in her arms, when the poor thing had to vomit, which made the old Colonel laugh; but he punished both her and her husband. It was this that made him leave the regiment.

Then we had plenty of men who made 'Bishops', a sort of bladder to fit into their shirt, inside their trowsers, to hold about 8[?] drams, and smuggle it out of the canteen. This way these men sold it to the other men, mostly at 'Gun Fire' in the morning at 5 a.m. This they called 'Gun Fire Tots'. We got it as we turned out to drill. These men would save a lot of money, and drink nothing for some time. This was called 'to put the bag on'. But when they did break out, they would drink to such an extent that they had mostly to go to hospital from the effects. At the time the *batta* money was served out there were about thirty men in hospital from drink. The Regimental Sergeant-major died; Sergeant-major Kelly died; Sergeant Jones and many of the privates died. The drink did more for death than the fever or other complaints.

Soon after our arrival in Ambala, the 14th Light Dragoons[a] came from Kirkee, Bombay. They were too late for the campaign, and got no *batta* or medal. This regiment was commanded by Lieutenant-colonel Havelock [see p. 136], and had to do part of their work,[b] which brought on fever. They buried two or three men every week, out of about 600 men, which told on their ranks. When they first came to Ambala they buried their dead with military honours, the Band, and 'Saul's Dead March', the men in full dress; but when the hot weather set in they, like us, left it off, only sending a mounted party to follow. The blacks carried the dead in dhoolies, a sort of covered stretcher.

Our regiments were made up to 700 strong each. The 16th

[a] The 14th was founded in 1715, and known by the names of its Colonels till 1776. In that year it became 'The 14th Light Dragoons'. From 1830 to 1861 it was called 'The 14th (The King's) Light Dragoons'. From 1861 till 1920, when it was amalgamated with the 20th Hussars, its title was 'The 14th (King's) Hussars'. The regiment had been stationed for 72 years in Ireland during the 18th century. In the Peninsular War it had served with distinction, particularly at Oporto in 1809 and at Fuentes de Onŏro in 1811. The 14th had been in India since 1841, and was to remain there till 1860. In the suppression of the Indian Mutiny, it was the only European cavalry regiment to go through the whole of the rigorous Central Indian campaigns.

[b] This perhaps means that the commanding officer made the men undertake tasks which in other regiments were done by natives.

Lancers were broken up to be sent to England after twenty-four years' service in this country. There was one man went home who came out with the regiment. We got 200 horses from them, and 240 men, volunteers. These men received 30 rupees to volunteer. The 14th Light Dragoons only got one man (named Self). This was because they had to do their own work, or part of it, and they were very tight in the Canteen Rules. The men marked off when they had three drams each of rum—quite enough—three-quarters of a pint nearly. I thought it a very good rule. The men were more sober than our men; but in these days drink was the rage in India.

The next cold season the two regiments, the 14th and the 3rd, used to brigade together. We were dressed alike, only their buttons said '14th Lt. Dragns' round them and ours said '3rd Light Dragns'. We very often had 1,300 horses on parade, both regiments all alike, a pretty sight, when in line. We had also the 1st Native Cavalry, 600 strong, which would give us 18 or 1900 horses on parade. The strength of the three regiments would be 2,000 horses: 3rd Light Dragoons, 701; 14th Light Dragoons, 700; Native Cavalry, 600. This number would make seven or eight regiments at home. The extra one man in our regiment was a sergeant who beat the silver kettle-drums, an honour granted us for taking the drums in battle somewhere in Spain.[a]

Our time was now spent very idly, as all drill was in the morning, and dismounted drill in the evening. As it was very hot in the day, we sat on our charpoy or bedstead and played

[a] Pearman's regimental history is a little hazy. Some of the regiment's records claim that the silver kettle-drums, which for many years were carried by the 3rd wherever it went, were captured at Aughrim in Ireland in 1691. It is almost certain, in fact, that they were taken at Dettingen in 1743. Replicas, always carried uncovered, are still prized by the regiment. (Farmer, H. G., 'Kettledrums as Trophies', *Journal of the Society for Army Historical Research*, XXVI [1948], 27–32.)

at cards, Back Gammon or Chess or anything that took our taste. In this way our time was passed. At other times I would read books, or set at the needle.

In the winter months I mostly went out with my gun, with a comrade named Daniel Lamden. This was after morning drill was over. I was very fond of roaming about the country and conversing with natives — a people I always found very kind if properly treated by us, but I am compelled to say some of our men used the poor native very bad. I recollect one day when out, we came in sight of a very large sort of deer, the Ellgie.[a] There were ten or twelve of them, not more than a hundred yards off. We both fired at them and killed one, a very fine female, but it was no use to us as we were eight or nine miles in a jungle and had nothing to carry it home, so we left it where it lay. It was nearly as large as an Alderney cow.

On another occasion we saw a wild sow and pigs, and knowing they were very spiteful, we got into a low tree and fired and killed one of the pigs and wounded two or three more. There was such a noise with the pigs and the old sow as you never heard. She would not leave the dead pig, and kept running to the bottom of the tree and then to the pig. We became alarmed for our safety, but after a time (more than an hour) she left, leaving us two pigs, one dead, the other we killed. We took them to barracks and cooked them ourselves as the native will not touch them or come near the flesh of the Suah or swine, it being unclean. It would break his caste. But the white man will eat anything, do anything (but serve God). Our caste is never broke.

And one thing I was very sorry to see oftimes when out on night patrol in the officers' lines and in our barracks. We would come across our Parson dead drunk. We would have

[a] Probably *nilghai*, an antelope common all over the plains of India.

Pearman's Sutlej
Campaign Medal
1845–6

Below: Sir Henry (later
Viscount) Hardinge,
Governor-General of
India, 1845

Left: Lieutenant-general Sir Joseph Thackwell

Right: Lieutenant-general Sir Harry Smith, bart.

Below: A trooper of the 16th Lancers fighting three Sikh foot soldiers, probably at Aliwal

him carried to his bungalow or dwelling house. The blacks would laugh and say as they carried him to his bungalow, 'White mans Potteree Bote utch ah adamy Good Man and very nice Bibby [wife].'[a] She was very pretty and fond of life, and this couple never missed a dance or a spree at the officers' mess. It was at these times we used to find him drunk. He would have been better away. At length he was sent to another station and we got an old Parson, a very good man, a Mr Whitehead. The men were very fond of him as he would sit in the hospital for hours with the sick and pray with them and never find any fault with our ways, only exhort us to pray to God. He had the good will of us all. This Parson took the next campaign with us — that is our division of the army.

The drinking continued as long as the money lasted. At the beginning of each month there was a scene of drunkenness as the men were paid the back pay for the past month, and then that had to be spent in drink.

About this time the steady men and non-commissioned officers started a Library and each member paid four annas each month. The Colonel gave us his support (and all the officers) and a number of books to start with, and sent us newspapers — a very great luxury in those days. And the Colonel caused a Coffee room to be opened at 'Gun-fire' (5 a.m.), and hot coffee was ready at that hour — a capital thing for the men as we turned out to our Field Drill at 'Gun-fire'. Beside coffee you could get anything to eat you might want. This was when Lieutenant-colonel Lockwood [see p. 137] commanded the regiment. The Library had a good effect and in a few months half the men belonged to it. They were allowed to take the book to their own beds where they could lay and read. This kept the men from cards and drink, and very much improved their conduct.

[a] *Padri bahut achcha admi* — 'White man's padre very good man and very nice lady.'

We remained at Ambala for two years and six months
[April 7th, 1846, to Sept. 27th, 1848]. There had been a
stone laid for the foundation of a church. A number of coins
and papers were placed under it, but as we went on a campaign, the church was not gone on with, and some of the
brave lads who had been sent back with wounds (from different regiments) took a liking to the bottle that contained
the coins and its contents, so they got some gunpowder and
raised the stone. When the troops came back they found it
gone and the stone some few hundred yards off.

While the drinking with the *batta* money was going on,
some of our men took it into their heads to turn 'Blue Lights'
—that is ranters—and had a small chapel built, and made
more cry than wool in it.[a] Well, some other 'Holy Boys' took
it into their heads that the chapel stood in the way, and laid
some gunpowder under the chapel, and when the 'Blue
Lights' were going in, up went the chapel—and such a smoke
and dust! Well, of course, nobody did it, and it was never
found out. I must say these men called 'Blue Lights' were
some of the worst men in the regiment. They had made away
with their all for drink, and would then turn 'Blue Lights', a
term for men of this stamp. The natives said the 'Blue Lights'
were Mud Wallah Caste, drinking religion.

I spent most of my spare time in the jungle and small bush
wood with my gun, and our enjoyment in barracks was such
as any young man could like. We had books to read, cards to
play, Draught Boards, Chess Boards, Back Gammon, and
outside the barracks we had skittles and cricket, and once a
month we had a *Bon Ton* (dance) and all the females of the
station invited to it—half-caste and all, so long as they were
wife of a soldier.

[a] From the proverbial saying 'great cry and little wool', expressing derisive
contempt for him that promises much, but achieves little.

CHAPTER III

W ELL, things went on in this way until September 1848, when there were rumours of the Bengal army taking the field for a campaign. The native force at Multan under Sher Singh had deserted our side and gone over to the enemy who was in the fortress of Multan, which place the British troops had laid siege to for some months — all the hot weather. But now they had to entrench themselves as this 6,000 had deserted our side with their general (Rajah Sher Singh).

Here Pearman refers to the isolated local revolt which took place at Multan in April 1848. By the end of the summer it had turned into a rebellion of the whole Sikh nation against the British paramount power.

Gough, who had received a barony after his victory at Sobraon, had always realized that a second instalment of the war was unavoidable. The Sikhs and the Khalsa had been humbled but not destroyed. Ironically it was almost certainly the reforming energies of Henry Lawrence, the Resident at Lahore, which hastened the second Sikh War. That remarkable man's attacks against unjust taxes, cruel punishments, female infanticide and *suttee*, probably pleased the mass of the people, but to the men of influence, the *sardars*, these reforms were threats to their power.

To meet the crisis there was a new Governor-General, the Earl of Dalhousie (see p. 133). To him, as soon as war was seen to be inevitable, Gough insisted that he required no less than 24,000 men and 78 guns for a successful and final invasion of the Punjab. For four months Dalhousie resisted Gough's demands; but, convinced at last of the need, he gave way. The formation of 'The Army of the Punjab' speedily followed.

On September 27th, 1848, as we sat in our barracks at Ambala about 11 o'clock in the morning, a camel came trotting into the cantonments and in a great hurry inquired for the Brigadier's quarters, and was directed by the sentry to our Guard. As this seldom took place it put us all on the look out. At 1 o'clock it sounded 'Orders', and then came the news so long looked for: the 3rd King's Own to pack their boxes and take them to store rooms, and our kit and horse to be in marching order; the regiment to march at 3 o'clock in the afternoon. Women and children were to take up one barracks, and several sick men (convalescents) to be left with them. Poor children and mothers! Some of them took the last look at their fathers and husbands, but they bore it as a soldier's wife should.

Well, 3 o'clock came and there we sat, as fine a regiment of young men, 697 strong, as England could wish for. We gave a loud Hurra [*sic*] to the women as we marched off, to cheer the poor things, and off we went at a trot, not pulling up a rein until we were several miles off, for fear the women should follow. Two of them did, although we marched fifteen miles, and stopped that night in the tents with their husbands. How they got back I cannot say.

We continued our march until we came to Mudki. Here we halted three days for the infantry and some foot artillery. Our camp now came up to 7,000 men. We then marched to Ferozepur where we joined more of the army. We had to cross the river Sutlej, and took our route to Lahore, which we reached in the first week in November. Now we were

20,000 strong, all arms. We then crossed the river Ravi and made for Jullundur.

> At the earliest possible moment, Gough had sent Cureton forward with a mixed force to the north of Lahore, so as to cover the capital. It consisted of the 3rd and the 14th Light Dragoons, two native cavalry regiments, one infantry brigade, three troops of Horse Artillery and one light field battery. On November 2nd this force encamped at Parhal, having crossed the Ravi. Gough followed as quickly as he could, with a large part of the army. He was anxious to attack the enemy as soon as possible, so as to prevent too large a concentration against him.

In the morning we all marched about 8 a.m. And now to find the enemy, and, as the boys would say, to get *batta* or prize money. Rajah Sher Singh was with his army at the town of Wazirabad (about 60,000 men), and we made for that place which is on the bank of the river Chenab about 70 miles north of the city of Lahore. Our army at this time was under the command of Lieutenant-general Cureton.

On November 5th we came in sight of a small party of the enemy that had been sent to look out for us, and we had a smart gallop after them, our Horse Artillery keeping along side of us. But as their horses appeared fresh, and we had made a long march, we could not come up to them. There was one of their men killed.

We formed camp here and waited two days for General Sir Joseph Thackwell. But the enemy changed their camp, and went about thirty miles down the river Chenab to a town called Ramnagar. Our army then changed its front and took ground to the north-west and halted about ten miles from the enemy's camp. Here we remained waiting for the main army and the Commander-in-Chief, Sir Hugh Gough, who came in on November 20th, 1848, and we were not left idle long. When he came he had an inspection of the whole army on general parade, and spoke a lot of stuff to us of the laurels to be gained for our country, and honour to the regiment, but not a word about the pension you would get if you got cut about.

To say the truth, we had not been idle before he came, for we were on our horses half the twenty-four hours. We had a double chain of infantry vedettes, and in advance of them, the cavalry, two men every hundred yards, with orders at night to fire on anyone coming from the front. When we were in-lying picquet we never took a thing off man or horse, and the whole army turned out one hour before daylight every morning, the infantry to stand to arms, the cavalry mounted, the artillery with guns loaded and match lit. We remained like this for an hour after daylight, and then filed into camp. After the horses had been fed, and ourselves, we had (that is a part of us) every few hours to patrol and reconnoitre the enemy. So we were not very idle.

We now began to look forward to a general engagement. On the morning of November 22nd, 1848, we were very comfortable in camp, and all off duty, I should think asleep. At 4 o'clock in the morning an order was given that the first division of the army would dress immediately and turn out without noise to reconnoitre the enemy's camp and their positions, under the charge of Major-general Cureton. The first division was about 8,000 strong, most of it cavalry and 12 guns.[a] It was very dark when we marched, and the dust made it worse, so we went very slow in two small columns, the guns in the centre.

About 8 o'clock we came in sight of the enemy's outposts.

[a] Besides the cavalry there were an infantry brigade under Brigadier Colin Campbell and three batteries of horse artillery.

These were to the south of the river, scattered about on the hard plain between Ramnagar and the river bank. The main Sikh force, perhaps 16,000 strong, with twenty-eight guns, was in position to the north of the river with easily negotiated fords in its front.

Gough was anxious to discover the strength of the enemy opposed to him. At the same time he 'deemed it necessary to attack the force [on the south side of the river] before it could get across the Chenab'[9] to join the main Sikh army. Thus what started as a reconnaissance developed into the action of Ramnagar.

The sun had risen and got bright through the dust. The 3rd Light Dragoons were ordered to advance and drive in the enemy's outposts. It sounded 'Trot', and we had to jump a nullah [one of the dry watercourses which intersected the plain], and then get down the deep bank. It then sounded 'Gallop', and at them we went, but they showed us their backs, leaving their tents behind them. Down to the river they went, and us after them, neck or nothing, but they took the ford and joined their army, which lay quiet enough but was soon on the alert.

We halted on the bank of the river, about half a mile from the enemy with the river between us. We waited some time until the remainder of the division came up. General Cureton came with them. He gave the order for our first squadron [under Lieutenant Ouvry] to break ranks and gallop up [along] the bank of the river to see how many guns the enemy could bring to bear on us as we went. So off we went, broke up like a lot of sheep, only farther apart. We had not gone far when 'Bang!' went their guns at us as we galloped for about three miles. We were told that they fired 67 guns at us. We had six or seven horses cut down, but the men were not hurt. I saw Sergeant Wood's horse shot, and

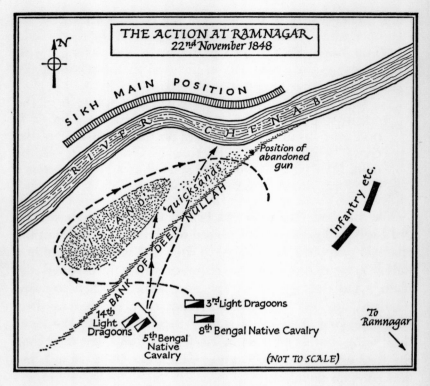

THE ACTION AT RAMNAGAR
22nd November 1848

SIKH MAIN POSITION

RIVER CHENAB

ISLAND

'quicksands'

BANK OF DEEP NULLAH

Position of
abandoned
gun

Infantry etc.

14th
Light
Dragoons

5th Bengal
Native
Cavalry

3rd Light Dragoons

8th Bengal Native Cavalry

To
Ramnagar

(NOT TO SCALE)

Privates Poole's and Wooders', in about three minutes. Jack Alder was in front of me twenty yards. I saw the gun ready and they were lighting the match. I said 'Look out, Jack!' A round shot came and cut the pouch from the belt at his back, but did not touch him. At this time we were riding over quicksands, and some of the horses got set fast, up to the belly. The men had to leave them.

By this time a party of the enemy horse with lances came in our rear. One was behind me. My horse was nearly beat, but I formed a right rear guard with my sword to parry off his lance should he point, as he was only about six feet from me. We kept like that some distance. My horse at this time could

72

only go about six miles an hour, but the lancer did not close up with me. Private William Hacken was behind him and he put his sword through him, putting a stop to his gallop. Hacken was well mounted and came alongside of me and said 'Jack, that chap meant to have you if your horse failed.' At this moment a shot struck in front of us and nearly brought us to the ground, but better luck.

On we went, and as soon as we were clear of them we brought our horses to a walk and most of us got together again. We took ground to the left and in about half an hour found our three squadrons of the regiment drawn up near a nullah and very close to a tope of trees. We called the roll of our squadron and seventeen men and horses were missing.

While Ouvry's squadron of the 3rd was thus at work, the horse artillery guns were ordered forward, probably so as to cover Ouvry's withdrawal. As the guns approached the water's edge, they, like the 3rd, found the ground soft and muddy. After they had fired several rounds, they limbered up and retired to a better position. In so doing one of the guns got stuck. After nearly an hour's ineffectual struggle, all the while under fire from the Sikh artillery concealed on the river's high north bank, the gun had to be abandoned. This misfortune, and the apparent retreat of Ouvry's men, so excited the Sikhs that they recrossed the fords with considerable numbers of horsemen and infantry, and even, it is thought, brought some of their guns on to a prominent 'island' between two dry watercourses.

The enemy had now come out in great force and crossed the river to our side, and the battle began in right earnest. Here we sat for nearly an hour, their infantry firing at us. They did not do us much harm, although the shot went 'tit tit' round and by you, very fast. Several men were shot and many horses wounded. The right of the regiment now fell back near the trees to try to draw out the enemy, but no go. They kept to the nullah. We again formed line and made two feint charges, but could not get them out. We now went back to the trees again, as we saw the 14th Light Dragoons coming down, their horses being fresh, not having done anything but the steady march in the morning.

It is difficult to discover exactly what happened next. That it was unnecessarily calamitous there can be no doubt. Gough himself had not intended to interfere with the 'reconnaissance', but when he was told about the stranded gun, he rode forward to see if it could be extricated. After a considerable time he found Cureton who was 'in front of the 14th Light Dragoons, and not under fire'. The Colonel of the 14th, William Havelock, now rode up to Cureton 'and asked permission', in Gough's presence, 'to charge a body of the enemy's cavalry, which appeared to be close .... Leave was given to him .... To my astonishment', wrote Gough, 'Havelock took his Regiment, with a portion of the 5th [Native] Cavalry, in Column of Troop, right down to the river, when he wheeled into line, and charged along the whole face of the Sikh batteries at the opposite side.'[10]

This is the Commander-in-Chief's much telescoped description of what happened. 'One who was present' told William Havelock's more famous brother Henry, that Gough himself had said to William: 'If you see a favourable opportunity of charging, charge.'[11] Captain Apthorp, the 14th's Adjutant, had no doubt that 'Havelock thought this almost tantamount to an order', since Gough had apparently said to Cureton that he could not understand 'a dry nullah stopping cavalry'. Havelock, leaving one squadron of his regiment in reserve, set off 'happy as a lover' with the other three.[12]

The 14th came on in pretty style, so steady and straight; but Colonel Havelock knew nothing of the nullah in their front, full of the enemy's infantry. Our Colonel, Michael White, called out 'Havelock! Havelock!' and pointed to the nullah, but on they went. Then came a volley and smoke. The 14th Light Dragoons had gone down into the nullah and over the enemy infantry. The poor fellows had some hard work. I saw David Todd come back. I knew him. He was covered with blood. Then more came back. Poor Todd didn't go far. A shot came and knocked off his head. Colonel Havelock was killed and between twenty and thirty men.

Soon after, General Cureton came down with the staff, and went to find Colonel Havelock, when a shot struck him. He threw up his arms and life was gone. Also the Colonel of the 1st Native Cavalry on the staff was shot at the same time. We buried them next day like soldiers with their cloaks round them, all in one grave at the village of Ramnagar.

The full story of this tragic incident, so graphically described by Pearman, is as follows: Cureton had been told by White, who had charged with Ouvry's squadron of the 3rd, about the dangers of the nullah and the 'quicksands' beyond it. He was horrified, therefore, to see that Havelock, having speedily driven back the enemy horse in his first advance, did not do as the 3rd had done, and resist the temptation to go further.

Gough thought that Havelock had lost 'the direction of the body of Gorchurras [Sikh irregular horsemen] which General Cureton had sanctioned his attacking', and had charged in error 'across one arm of the river, under the bank of which numbers both of infantry and cavalry were concealed'. Cureton, appalled at the blunder about to be committed, exclaimed, it is said: 'My

God! This isn't the way to use cavalry!'[13] He at once rushed forward, with a small escort of the 5th Native Cavalry, to try to stop Havelock, but he had gone only a short distance when he was shot dead by a matchlock ball.[a] Havelock and fourteen of his men were killed, and five officers and twenty-two men wounded.

The general consensus of opinion is that Havelock lost his head. 'It was natural', wrote his brother, 'that an old Peninsular officer, who had not seen a shot fired since Waterloo, should desire to bleed the noses of his young dragoons.'[14] On the other hand if it is true that Gough 'pooh-poohed'[15] White's and Cureton's advice about the dangers of the nullah and the 'quicksands' — and it would seem to have been in character for him to do so — the Commander-in-Chief was guilty of inciting Havelock to rashness. This would have been especially reprehensible, since not more than six or seven of the men of the 14th had ever seen action before.

Our artillery was drawn up near the nullah and was making good practice on the enemy. The infantry had also got at work, and death was gathering in his harvest in good earnest. I could only see now and again what was going on, but as the enemy outnumbered us we had to change our position very often.

The day was now getting advanced, and the sun showed signs of putting an end to the dreadful sight, so the army formed itself into battle order for the morrow and returned to bivouac for the night. At the same time the Sikhs crossed the river, having had enough of it themselves.

Thus ended the unhappy affair of Ramnagar. Henry Havelock (who was not present) neatly summed up the

---

[a] It is difficult to be certain who was killed first, Cureton or Havelock. Pearman (*see above*) says that it was Havelock. Other eye-witnesses suggest that it was Cureton.

mistakes of the day. The Sikh horse, 'pushed forward on the left [south] bank, were intended', he wrote, 'to bravado and decoy, and should have been simply let alone, or cannonaded when convenient and possible, by guns out of reach of those of the enemy.'[16]

Gough had certainly achieved his intention of clearing the south bank, and numbers of the enemy had been killed, but the price had been ridiculously high. The death of Cureton, India's foremost cavalry commander, was a real tragedy.

We had a very hard day and man and horse wanted rest, but we had nothing to eat. The horses had been without food or water from the night before, and nothing for them now. We dare not give them water as they had nothing to eat. I had some arrack or rum in my bottle, so I made a drink, and myself and horse shared it. (It was so dark!) The men began to look after anything they could get to eat. I gave my horse to another to hold, so did my comrade (William Makepiece) and we went to look for something. The artillery had found a dead man of theirs in a house near Ramnagar—about sixty or seventy houses in a lump, clear of the large town—and these we looted.

Myself, Makepiece and Dick Curtis got a small bullock and took it to our bivouac. We killed it with a sword through the body and made a fire. It was soon eaten, the men taking a bit as they could get it, and cooked it at the fire. Bread we had none, but I made a good meal on the half-cooked meat, so was much better off than my poor horse. I lay down on the ground to try to sleep, my horse's reins over my arm. I had snatched a few winks when some of the men called out 'the houses are on fire!' Some of the artillery, it was said, set fire to them. They were burnt down. I don't know what became of the people. As the men fell asleep, they let their horses loose, which made great confusion, and caused us to get up and swear, just as we had dropped off to sleep.

Morning came, and with daylight our tents, cooks and commissary, so we got corn and fed our horses after thirty-six hours' fast and sixteen hours' ride. We then fed ourselves, put up our tents, watered the horses, had our grog, and lay down, and soon forgot all in sleep. After thirty-six hours without food or water, the horses wanted much looking after, but our black servants took to them well. I had a good man, very fond of the horse, and when he saw he was not hurt, he patted and made much of him, and the poor brute seemed to know it for he squealed and seemed to thank him for what he got. In the morning we went over the battlefield, and buried the dead.

Duty now became very hard on us: on duty at morning, on duty again at night, and in the day we had to patrol the enemy's positions. About midday on November 27th we had to turn out in a hurry. The enemy had stole a march on us, and taken several thousand camels belonging to us that were out to feed in the jungles in care of their keepers. We galloped many miles after them, but they had gone too far and there was a small army between them and us. All we got was a few shots for our trouble. We returned to camp tired but none the worse.

On November 30th, 1848, Lord Gough came and took charge of the camp, which at this time was between 20 and 30 thousands strong, with 64 guns, 12 of them heavy ones.

> After the unhappy affair at Ramnagar, Cureton's place at the head of the cavalry was taken by Thackwell, who was also made second-in-command of the army. On December 2nd, with a large detached force (which Pearman refers to as 'the first division'), Thackwell crossed the Chenab unopposed near Wazirabad. Gough

intended him to march down the north bank of the river and to attack the left of the Sikh position at Ramnagar, while Gough held the enemy's attention with an artillery barrage. The plan miscarried, and Thackwell fought a minor and inconclusive action at Sadulapur on December 3rd.

The first division of the army to which I belonged received orders to march at one o'clock in the morning of December 1st, to Wazirabad, a large town on the banks of the river Chenab, about thirty miles from Ramnagar. Our strength was 8,000 men and 34 guns, with orders to cross the river and come up on the other side of the river so as to steal a march on the enemy. We arrived at the town of Wazirabad at dark on the night of the 1st, having marched the thirty miles. We had no tents and we lay that night on the sand on the river edge near the ford, and when we had got our grog, half a pint of arrack, and some cold meat and bread, we lay down to rest, but not to sleep, for the water came through the sand and made our cloaks wet which made us very cold; but we dozed off at times and had a little sleep. We were very glad when daylight came and got our breakfast: cold meat and bread and half a pint of arrack and plenty of water.

About 8.30 a.m., December 2nd, the enemy's outposts came out to reconnoitre us, but kept away from the river. There was only about one regiment of them. We received the order to undress, take off our boots, draws and trowsers, tie them round our necks and then mount our horses to take the ford, which we did in file or by twos, a row of camels above stream and a row below us. So into the water we went, and cold it was, most of it snow water from the Kashmir mountains. The river was about 1,000 yards wide. Some of the horses lost their line and had to swim. We got over without any lost, and drove away the enemy. Then the infantry crossed in boats with the guns. By 10 a.m. we had all of us on the enemy's side of the river, and commenced our march up the side until it got dark, feeling our way as we went, halting at times and sending out small parties to look for any of the enemy that might show themselves.

At night we lay among some turnips and carrots, of which we eat and gave our horses. We got cold meat and bread, half a pint of arrack, and lay down for the night. After placing our guard and outposts at daylight we got our grog, meat and bread, and commenced the march. About midday we lay down to rest, sending out some guns and our Grey Squadron (or left squadron) to look out for the enemy.

We must have laid down nearly an hour. I was fast asleep, my head on my shako, my horse's reins in my swivel on the belt, when a Private Jack Alder shook me and said, 'Damn you, corporal. Wake up! Here comes the enemy.' At that moment two round shot passed very playfully by us, and away they went. We were soon into the saddle and into Troops. In a few minutes our infantry were on their feet and in close column of companies, the artillery moving very quietly to the front. The guns sent out with the Grey Squadron had now opened fire, covered by the Grey Squadron. They were now slowly falling back to us, but in such lovely order, like a field day.

Our little army now formed line to meet them, although we could see they were four times as many as us. We were under the command of Major-general Sir Joseph Thackwell with his one arm. Our regiment was commanded by Lieutenant-colonel Yerbury, 'old black jack' [see p. 139]. As soon as the Grey Squadron joined the regiment, the guns formed in our line and continued the fire, the infantry laying down in line to escape the enemy's long shot. The left of their line at this time began to outflank ours, and we were ordered to

The Battle of Aliwal, January 28th, 1846: one of the charges made by
the 16th Lancers

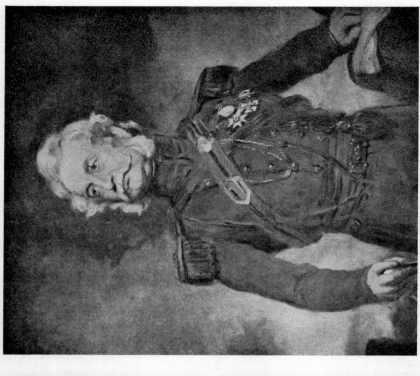

Field-Marshal Hugh, Viscount Gough, Commander-in-Chief, India, Brig.-gen. C. R. Cureton in the uniform of the 16th Lancers; by Sir Francis Grant killed at Ramnagar (see p. 75)

Field-marshal Hugh, Viscount Gough, Commander-in-Chief, India: pencil
sketch for portrait in oils by Sir Francis Grant (*see opposite*)

try a feint charge, which we did, but it had no effect to turn their flank. We were then ordered to throw our right back by echelon, which was done at a gallop, and when our line came to front it was a great surprise to the enemy, for our right now out-flanked them by half a mile, which caused them to halt.

They had a great number of cavalry on their left, which fronted my regiment. At this time our guns were doing a good practice. There was in our left front a sugar cane plantation which was filled with their infantry, and into this our guns fired grape and canister and killed a great number, as we saw them lying dead after the battle. Our line now began to turn the tables on them, for we had the order to advance. I could see the 9th Lancers had got across the river, also some of the infantry, which made the enemy turn and retreat. The sun was just going down, so we gave them a few parting shots and let them go. There was the village of Sadulapur between us and the enemy, and the people stood on the top of the houses to see the fight, although the shot and shell went over their head, backwards and forwards from their and our guns.

We were told that while the fight was going on, Lord Gough was left on the other side of the river with the main army, about seven miles off, and could not get boats to get across. It was said that he stamped and swore, and ran to and fro like mad, until they found a ford in the river and got to our relief. The battle lasted about four hours. Our loss was but small. At night we bivouacked on the ground with nothing to eat and nothing for our poor horses. We could not get water.

About 8 o'clock p.m. I with several others (Dick Curtis, Topley, Makepiece, Baxter and one or two more) went in search of something to eat. We went to the village, where the poor people put up their hands, and begged of us not to hurt them. We had our sword blades drawn. We did not mean to hurt them. We only wanted food. At length we found a young cow, about half grown, and we drove it towards our horses, but the fool would not go, so we tied its legs and put a pole through them, and carried it back downwards to our Troop. The boys had made a fire, so now came the tale how to kill it, and cook some. But while this was going on, Ike Stag run his sword through the beast, and before it was dead, he was cutting a slice off its rump. We soon all fell to, and got some sticks and we toasted it at the fire and eat it half done as so many got round the fire with pieces. Some other men got some fowls; some got a goat and a sheep, so in a short time we had made a supper on meat, and we had got our grog, so we took our horses' reins, put them on our belt swivel and lay down to sleep. I can say that I slept well, nothing disturbed in mind or body about stealing the young cow.

At daybreak next morning we were on the move after the enemy, leaving a few behind to bury the dead and see to the wounded; but when we got near the ford at Ramnagar, the enemy had all moved off, and was a day's march in advance of us, but we continued to follow up their rear and annoy them with our skirmishers the whole day. At night we encamped about ten miles from the enemy, but they got on the move in the night and in the morning they were all gone, and their rear guards were out of sight.

Our army continued to advance until we came to a place named Helan, and here we pitched our camp. The next day Lord Gough came up with the main army. Then we had a standing camp for a month. Duty was rather hard: a great many on duty at the same time; out-lying picquets and in-lying picquets, and a squadron to reconnoitre every day for several days; the whole army to sleep in arms. But when off duty we had plenty of sports such as races, jumping in sacks, jumping the High Leap and any kind of sport that was to be thought of, the officers and men mixing together. The officers do not have so much pride on Service.

While we lay in this camp we got everything comfortable and plenty of it, and occasionally some bottled beer. We marched from this camp, Helan, on January 11th, 1849, and encamped in a pretty place, plenty of pea fowl and the ground well looked to, and the people seemed happy. On the 12th we marched again, most of the day in a jungle, but now and then there was a small village. At night we encamped on a plain and could hear the guns of the enemy, as if they had been at drill in the evening before sundown.

The long delay between the indecisive action at Sadulapur on December 3rd, 1848, and the resumption of hostilities in mid-January 1849, was caused by a prohibition imposed upon Gough by Dalhousie. This prohibition was connected with questions of supplies, supports and communications, with doubts as to whether the army was strong enough for the task ahead, and with the siege of Multan. This, which had been carried on, intermittently, since September, was tying up a mixed force of Bengal and Bombay troops, which would have been useful to the Commander-in-Chief. Yet before the eventual fall of Multan, on January 22nd, and before, therefore, any considerable reinforcements could reach Gough, other considerations induced Dalhousie to give him the go-ahead. Chief among these was the fact that considerable reinforcements were about to reach the Sikhs, including troops from Afghanistan. With every week of delay not only did the enemy's strength increase, but so also did his self-confidence.

On the morning of January 13th, 1849, never to be forgot,

we marched at 5 a.m. and with a strong party of cavalry skirmishers to the front. I was at this time attached to the Grey Squadron although I belonged to A Troop, the Black Troop. The 3rd, or King's Own Light Dragoons was as follows, that is: C and H Troops were all bay horses, the 1st or right Squadron. F Troop: chestnut horses; G Troop: dun horses. This was the 2nd Squadron. E Troop was pied and skewball horses; A Troop black horses. This made the 3rd Squadron. B and D Troops, all grey horses. This was the 4th or left Squadron. There were therefore eight Troops or four Squadrons. Each Troop sent out six men to skirmish from the flanks of the squadron. Our regiment numbered at this time about 600 men on duty, but some of these were on rearguard, in charge of the treasure. The Squadrons would be about 120 rank and file each when we were in the front of the enemy this day.

We marched until about 10 o'clock in the morning, when it sounded 'Halt' and we stood as we were. When it sounded the halt some of us got off our horses. I had been out skirmishing and it had not sounded for skirmishers to come in, although we could see our people putting in the small flags for our camp ground. A man named Dick Brown had been a little way farther into the jungle than the rest of us, and came back and said there were a lot of the enemy behind the village; but Sergeant Small came out with our bread and grog at this time, so I told him what Brown had seen, and he went back to tell the Colonel of the regiment, but he had not left many minutes when two 6-pound shot passed over our head, and in the direction of the staff and Lord Gough, and this got the old man's Irish out; for in a few minutes more, 'Bang' went the guns at His Lordship's side in return for theirs. We now got into our saddles, when it sounded 'Skirmishers in,' and the whole army prepared for battle.

85

This account by Pearman of how the battle of Chilianwala came about may not be far from the truth. Some
authorities believe that there was no real need to fight
on January 13th, and that had Gough been less impul-
sive, he could have gained a decisive victory next day.
Gough's own version is, of course, different. When he
advanced to Chilianwala, between which village and the
broad river Jhelum the main Sikh army was known to be
arrayed in a strong entrenched position, he intended
merely to make a reconnaissance, or at most, 'to fall
across the Sikhs should they attempt flight'.

From a mound about three miles from the enemy's
entrenchments he surveyed the scene. 'As it was one
o'clock before I fully satisfied myself of his position,' he
wrote in his diary, 'I determined to postpone the attack
until the following morning, and the Quartermaster-
General was in the act of arranging the formation of the
camp when the enemy brought forward some guns to
bear upon Chilianwala.' Gough at once ordered forward
his heavy artillery to dislodge them. This was soon
accomplished, but, in reply, the Sikh artillery opened up
'from nearly their whole line, evidently thrown much in
front of their different positions.'[17] Realizing that the
enemy had advanced from their entrenchments to the
edge of the jungle, Gough decided to attack at once. He
took this decision in spite of the lateness of the hour (not
much before 2 p.m.), and aware that his troops would
have to attack through 'a belt of rather dense low
jungle'.[18] It was certain that if he retired, the Sikhs
would advance. Further, there was no water to be had
except at Chilianwala. He therefore had no alternative,
he claimed, but to fight the battle there and then.

We took ground to the left, and then we saw plenty of the
enemy, who had been all the morning waiting for us, and they
came down very close to us; not further off than four or five

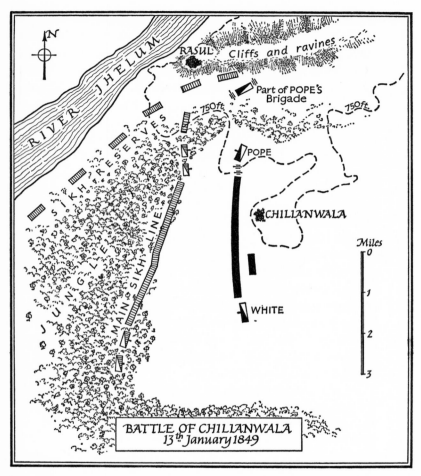

BATTLE OF CHILIANWALA
13th January 1849

hundred yards, mostly cavalry in front of us, but we could see
their infantry in their rear. By this time we had been at it
about an hour. It commenced about 11 o'clock a.m., but the
artillery had done a lot of work and still kept it up. The
right of our army, near three miles from us, had most of it at
this time, but at 1 o'clock p.m. they pressed our left centre
very much, and came down in columns of three or four

thousands strong. About half a mile from us on our right was H.M. 24th Foot.[a] Next to them were the 15th Sepoys[b] on their left between them and us, but between these two regiments was Captain Christie's Troop of Bengal Horse Artillery. The whole was in a thick bush. In our front was the most plain ground, but that had plenty of low bushes.

The battle which now began in earnest was largely an infantry and artillery affair. The nature of the ground precluded the extensive use of the cavalry. The enemy line, spread thinly over six miles, greatly outflanked Gough's at both ends. In it were some 30,000 men with over sixty guns. Its left was unassailable, being placed at Rasul among steep cliffs and numerous ravines. The British force did not number more than 14,000 men with sixty-six guns.

Thackwell placed himself with White's cavalry brigade on the left of the line. White commanded the 3rd Light Dragoons and two native cavalry regiments. On the right of the line were the 9th Lancers, 14th Light Dragoons and two further native regiments, under Brigadier Alexander Pope.

As the infantry plunged into the jungle, each brigade (of which there were four in line and one in reserve) 'lost its neighbour', as the Governor-General wrote to the Duke of Wellington. 'Every regiment was separated from the one next to it, and fought a battle for itself.'[19] Both the high casualties (mostly in the infantry) and the

[a] Formed in 1689, the 24th (as it became in 1751) was renamed the 24th (2nd Warwickshire) Regiment of Foot in 1782. In 1881 it became the South Wales Borderers. Its battle honours include 'Egypt and the Sphinx' (1801), seven from the Peninsular War, Chilianwala and Gujrat.

[b] This regiment, 'the Regiment of Ludhiana', had been raised in 1846 after the first Sikh War. It consisted of Sikhs recruited on the left bank of the Sutlej, and served with loyalty and distinction in the second Sikh War. In 1861 it was brought into the line as the 16th, and, later in the year, as the 15th Bengal Native Infantry. In 1885 it became the 14th Bengal Infantry.

inconclusiveness of the action are partly explained by Pearman's penetrating observation that

The enemy had chosen a rare place for us to work. We could not combine one [infantry] regiment to the other, so close was the jungle in places.

About 2 o'clock p.m. there was a great deal of fighting about the centre. H.M. 14th Light Dragoons went threes about and went back into the rear, right by and over the General Hospital, and so did one wing of the 9th Lancers, but they came about again, and back into the line. This left a great opening in the centre, and the enemy's cavalry came down on the 24th Foot, and, poor fellows, how they did fight with the bayonet! The Troop of guns of Captain Christie's was also taken from us and nearly all killed. Captain Christie was killed, and the poor 15th Sepoys stood until they were nearly all killed.

This disastrous phase of the battle, here laconically and not entirely accurately described by Pearman, occurred on the right of the British line. It did not therefore, of course, come under his personal observation.

What actually happened was that Brigadier Pope, when he saw the infantry on his left attacking, ordered his nine squadrons[a] to mount, deploy and advance. This they did, two squadrons of the 9th Lancers on the right, three native squadrons in the centre, and the four squadrons of the 14th on the left. They moved in one long line with ten horse artillery guns between them and the infantry. Not a single skirmisher was placed in front, nor was there a single man left in support or reserve. An officer of the 14th relates that Pope himself led the

[a] Pope, earlier on, seeing a considerable force of Sikh horsemen on the hills threatening his right, had detached five squadrons and eight guns to keep them off. These, except for protecting the right flank, took no further part in the battle.

line from the centre, and that before long he 'came to a dead halt at the sight of a few Sikh horsemen .... The Sikhs seeing the hesitation, a handful of their horsemen, some forty or fifty in a lump, charged boldly into the thick of the native cavalry, who instantly turned with the cry "Threes about", and disappeared for the rest of the day.'[20] The panic communicated itself to the 9th and to a lesser degree to the 14th, and in due course to the horse artillery, which found itself, on the disappearance of the cavalry, wholly unprotected. The Sikh horsemen, exultantly following up, cut down many of the gun teams, carried off four guns, and put out of action another six. Pope himself was mortally wounded in the retreat, but the cavalry casualties were shamefully few.

The blame for the debacle rests with those responsible for appointing Pope to his command. He was so ill and enfeebled that he had to be lifted into the saddle. He had never commanded more than a squadron in the field before. It seems that even when bringing his brigade up before the battle, his irresolute inefficiency had been manifest. When he formed his nine squadrons in a single long line, leaving not a squadron in support, all confidence in him must have finally ebbed away. A more foolish formation, especially in a jungle with numerous obstructions, can hardly be imagined.

The right-hand infantry brigade, finding their flank totally exposed as a result of Pope's fiasco, had a hard time of it, but eventually, by skill and good luck, extricated itself from a perilous position.

At much the same time as this sorry episode was taking place on the right, a large force of Sikh cavalry, perhaps 800 strong, was advancing in an attempt to turn the British left.

My regiment was ordered to advance, the 4th Squadron to charge the enemy's right flank, which was getting round us.

The 5th Native Cavalry, which was our left regiment, was ordered to support the 4th Squadron and then to retire into line again, which they did well.

> Captain Unett (see facing p. 128), commanding the 4th ('Grey') Squadron, in which Pearman was, says that the 5th Native Cavalry 'ran away to a man'.[21] There is good evidence, however, to corroborate Pearman's statement, and to show that the 5th rallied with perfect steadiness on the 8th Native Cavalry, which Thackwell had held in reserve.[22] Nevertheless the Grey Squadron had to go on alone, the Sikh horsemen closing around it.

Well away we went, Captain Unett in front, and Lieutenant Stisted and Cornet Gough. Captain Unett shouted 'Come on, boys! Now for it!' But he was soon cut down, and so was Lieutenant Stisted, and young Gough was also on the ground, the first and second badly wounded. The enemy formed a complete wedge, and we had to cut our way through them for quite a hundred yards before there was any clear ground.

> The lieutenant commanding Unett's right-hand troop states that the Sikh horsemen now 're-formed their line on nearly the same ground on which we had just charged through them.'[23] Unett and his two fellow officers collected what men they could lay hands upon, and charged back again. This time the enemy 'did not offer so much opposition, but opened out, and abused us as we passed .... On our re-forming they retired off the field.'[24]

I believe the Colonel and the regiment did not think of seeing any of us again. As it was, forty-six were killed and wounded of the rank and file (twenty-six killed and twenty wounded in the charge, and most of that twenty died).

> These figures may be an exaggeration. Other sources state that only twenty-four officers and men were killed

91

and sixteen wounded. It is of interest to note that all accounts agree that more men were killed than wounded, a fact which illustrates how tight a spot the squadron was in. On re-forming there were seen to be only forty-eight men in their saddles, out of the 106 who had charged.

This dashing action of the 'Grey' squadron of the 3rd, which caused panic and dismay on the Sikh right, has been over-shadowed in most accounts of the battle by the unhappy performance of Pope's brigade on the British right.

I had a bayonet wound in the right arm as we cut our way back to the regiment—a slight flesh wound near the elbow. I have no other belief but the fellow would have shot me as my horse was plunging and my sword was in the fellow's shoulder, but Sergeant Wild coming up, cut off the back of his head, and down he went. Wild said 'Come on, Jack', and away we went, about seven of us, and got safe to the regiment, where I got a bandage put round my arm. What men got back, got back by three or five or six or seven at a time, some one way and some came another. I can never forget this charge. Such a mass to get through. How any of us did get back was a wonder. Captain Unett and Lieutenant Stisted were presented to the Queen after they returned to England, for their gallant conduct.

The battle lasted until dark at night, when both armies stayed on the ground, and the killed and wounded lay where they fell. Our small army lost about two thousand and the enemy it was said lost near five thousand, so what with men and horses, the place was covered with dead and dying. That night I prayed to God that I might never see that sight again. In the night it came on to rain, which did not improve our very nice condition, but we had to put up with it, and I am proud to say the men did not grumble about it. Sometimes they would wish they had some grog.

I forgot to say above that we took twelve of their guns, and they took six of ours. Captain Christie's Troop was nearly all killed. I believe two or three men and a boy were [the only ones] not killed. The 24th Foot suffered very much. I believe their loss was 450 men, 19 officers and one of the colours of the regiment. The 2nd Bengal European Regiment [in Gilbert's division] also suffered very badly. Their loss was nearly as bad as H.M. 24th Foot's. The 15th Regiment of Sepoys was nearly cut up: few men left. One of their officers came to us and asked the Colonel to send them help, but he dared not move the regiment without an order.

Well, as I said, night closed the sad sight, and the rain came down as if to cleanse us from our past sin, for I verily believe man was not made by God to kill his fellow man. It has become the order of man since, by our artificial life, and to keep the rank of nations.

The total British losses at Chilianwala were 602 killed, 1,651 wounded and 104 missing. An interesting sidelight upon these figures (the size of which much horrified contemporary opinion) is thrown by Gough's biographer. The proportion of killed, he states, was about five per cent of the whole force; of wounded about twelve per cent. Only 72 of the 1,651 were permanently disabled, while of the 624 wounded Europeans, 156 had returned to duty a fortnight after the battle.[25]

The Sikh casualties were said to be very high.

When the fighting ceased, the Sikhs retired upon the hills to their left. Gough 'could not pursue from want of daylight, and he could not hold his ground from want of water'.[26] After bringing in as many of the wounded as possible, but leaving his spiked guns for the enemy to collect, he retired to the village of Chilianwala.

The next morning I went out with James Regan to find his brother Owen who was killed. We buried him and many more that were found. Some of the men had lived the night through. The rain had washed the wounds as white as veal. Some had died but we could do no more than what we did. Some had to be left to their fate.

About 10 o'clock a.m. we came back to the regiment and got our breakfast, bread and coffee, and then we mounted our horses to reconnoitre the position of the enemy so as to know how matters stood, after which Lord Gough ordered a few of the regiments to change their position. The infantry had to throw up entrenchments to watch the enemy, as we were but a short distance from each other. The rain continued to come down for several days, which made the camp in a very bad state — mud in every place.

On the night of the 17th, there was such a stir in the camp. About midnight an elephant had become unmanageable and got loose. It ran through the whole camp, which caused great trouble to the soldiers. Our horses broke loose, and so did horses of other regiments and some of the artillery. The night being very dark we could not get them, but morning came and most of them were got together. At daylight I was on main guard, and what with the uproar and the rain, the main guard tent fell down on us that were inside, and the men swore the camp had gone mad, and would not put the tent up again. So we sat and laid about until all were wet to the skin. The new guard came on duty at 9 o'clock in the morning.

At 11 o'clock we had to start to bring in a convoy of corn. About 3,000 went on the road to meet the corn, as it was thought the enemy would try to intercept it on the way; but we got it in safe. Duty still continued very hard. The infantry suffered very much as they had to lie in the entrenchments, and as there had been a great lot of rain it made it very uncomfortable.

When the weather cleared up, and it got dry, it made the place much better. But it never was a very clean camp. So many dead laying about not buried, and dead horses and camels all made it worse. True the birds and jackals eat up a great deal, but then there was a lot laying about to make a very bad smell. We got our rations regular, and I must say very good under the circumstances.

On February 6th we went out to reconnoitre the enemy, and exchanged a few shots. I don't think there was anyone killed or wounded. On February 7th I had to patrol the front of the vedettes of the enemy's lines. When we were a short way down we had to go about three miles along their front to see what we could, and report the same to Colonel Fordyce of the Staff Corps. At times their sentries would fire at ours. In the day time they were only about two hundred yards from the vedettes of the 9th Lancers. The jungle which we had to go through was very thick in places. We had to march in single file. I had four privates with me: William Taylor (called 'Little Billy Taylor', as we had four William Taylors in the Troop), first; Richard Brown, second; Julius Cooper, third; and Thomas Thornit last. I was on the left. We had our carbines at the advance. I met General Sir Joseph Thackwell walking in the jungle, his black syce leading his horse. He said: 'Sergeant, you can go further into the jungle. As I have just come up and seen nothing of the enemy's outposts, I think they have been taken in.' So I gave the order 'Left incline', and we went about 150 yards farther into the jungle towards the enemy, but we had not got more than half a mile before we came right on the enemy's outlying picquet, and between them and their two vedettes on the look-out. At this part the jungle was very thick, but the enemy showed the white of their heels to us. They jumped on their horses and rode off at a gallop. William Taylor wanted to fire at them, but my orders were not to fire at them. If they fired at us we were not to return the fire, but to march slowly on our way, and report the same to Colonel Fordyce. On our arrival at Colonel Fordyce's camp, I found he had been watching us with his glass. He asked me why I went so close to the enemy and into their outpost. When I told him what General Thackwell said, he only laughed at the mistake. I then returned with the four men to my camp.

Camp life now became very hard: on duty night and day, reconnoitring the enemy, which kept us always in the saddle, with our boots on our feet and swords and belts on. Our feet swelled very much as we could not be allowed to change our boots for [it was] only a short time before we were mounted again. We had also to take charge of the camels while they fed on the bush in the jungle. As there were several thousands, it took a deal of trouble. There were parties of other cavalry regiments as well as ours. The native cavalry and all, took part of this duty.

*   *   *

The news of Chilianwala, when it reached Britain, caused extreme dismay. The government became alarmed, and Sir Charles Napier (see p. 108), reluctantly consenting, was at once bundled off to India to supersede Gough. But long before he arrived, the Commander-in-Chief had gloriously vindicated his reputation by ending the war with one decisive blow.

The day after Chilianwala, Gough intended to pursue what little advantage he had gained, but the heavy rain to which Pearman refers above made any sort of move impossible. The Sikhs, meanwhile, received considerable reinforcements in their entrenched position at Rasul.

Maharajah Gulab Singh, of Jammu and Kashmir (*see p.* 58)

Following page

(*a*) (*left*) Lieutenant-colonel 'Jacky' Smyth, 16th Lancers (*see p.* 41)

(*b*) (*right*) Lieutenant-colonel William Havelock, 14th Light Dragoons, killed at Ramnagar (*see p.* 62)

These included some Afghan horse, Dost Muhammad, the ruler of Afghanistan, having succumbed to the temptation to have a crack at the British by allying himself with the Sikhs. Gough wisely decided, before continuing the struggle, to await the arrival of his own reinforcements, which, after the fall of Multan on January 22nd, were hastening towards him.

The enemy, meanwhile, tried everything possible to induce Gough to fight a pitched battle, but he would not be drawn. He knew that the Sikhs could not long subsist in the barren country around Rasul, and that they would soon be compelled to take up a less impregnable position. 'By a careful exploration of the ground and by a series of masterly movements', as Lord Lawrence has justly put it, Gough prepared the way 'for as crowning a victory as ever smiled upon our arms in India.'[27]

By the time the Multan troops had joined him, five weeks after Chilianwala, the Sikhs had placed themselves in an unentrenched position on an open plain at Gujrat, near the Chenab, which was precisely what Gough wanted. Further, he had, at last, an army of almost exactly the size which he had long ago stipulated as necessary for the conquest of the Punjab.

The section of Pearman's narrative which follows describes his experiences during the weeks which led up to Gough's final victory.

At about the beginning of February 1849, it was reported that the fortress of Multan had been taken by the British troops, and that part of their army had been driven out and was making towards us. This caused Sher Singh to move his army more to the left. We put our right wing back, and extended our left for about two miles so as to cover their movements.

On February 17th we went out to reconnoitre their position. We came against a party of the enemy, when a sharp fire was opened on both sides, but to very little good. A lot of ammunition was wasted, and only to end in smoke; but one of the enemy's matchlock balls struck my saddle, which was a little too close to be pleasant.

Sher Singh now altered his plans and moved his army to Gujrat, a large town. I believe it to be the finest town in the Doab.[a] We closed our line in his front about one and a half miles apart. Here we waited until a part of the Multan army joined us on the evening of February 20th, 1849: the men of the 10th Foot and 60th Rifles, and some artillerymen. They all had plenty of money, and gave it away to us, as if it was of no use. We got grog some way or other and had a jolly evening, had a song, and told each other of our late battles.

But at 10 p.m. all our comfort came to an end. An order came round the tents for the men to join their own regiments, as the camp would move at 5 o'clock in the morning to attack the enemy. So we had a parting glass, shook hands and parted, some of the brave lads for ever. There was but little sleep that night. We lay on the ground, talking of home, old comrades dead, and the coming day, and who would see the sun again set. I fell asleep, but had not slept long when it was down with the tents and get mounted, which took us about twenty minutes.

The army soon got together, and at daylight, there we were, face to face with the enemy. The line of our army covered about six miles of the front in a zig-zag sort of order. The 14th Light Dragoons on the right, with the 4th Native Lancers. The 9th Queen's Lancers on the left, with Captain Jacob's Native Bombay Irregulars, our infantry and artillery

[a] A tract of land lying between two rivers, which, after running for some distance, unite. The district between the Chenab and the Jhelum rivers, for instance, is called the Jetch Doab.

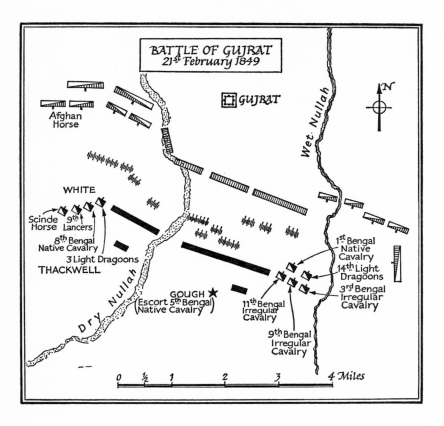

filling up the intervals. The 3rd Light Dragoons left centre, with the Scinde Irregular Horse, who carry matchlock guns and very long lances; a brave lot of men. In our front lay in ambush, in a corn field that was about two feet high (just enough to cover them), the 60th Rifles.

The fine town of Gujrat was in front of the centre of the army. About 7 a.m. our line began to advance towards the enemy's line, and we very shortly could hear the guns on the right hard at work on both sides. We closed up to about 800 yards.

To fight the battle of Gujrat, the preliminaries to which Pearman so graphically describes, Gough brought on to the field some 20,000 men with 88 guns, of which 18 were heavies. The enemy, though they may have had between 35,000 and 60,000 men, could produce only 59 guns. Thus, for the first time Gough possessed a marked superiority in artillery. This he used with great effect.

The battle opened with a massive gun duel which lasted from 9 a.m. till 11.30 a.m. The infantry then went in, and after some severe fighting, the Sikh army broke. Soon after 1 p.m. it was in headlong flight. 'We stood two hours in hell,' said one Sikh, 'and after that we saw six miles of infantry.'[28]

On Gough's flanks were three cavalry brigades. White commanded that on the left, overseen by Thackwell, who, as second-in-command of the army, took charge of all the troops to left of centre. Brigadier John Hearsey (see p. 137) commanded his own and Lockwood's brigades on the right. The 3rd Light Dragoons were in White's brigade.

Throughout the battle large numbers of the enemy's cavalry tried to turn the two flanks. Hearsey, by skilful use of his horse artillery, and cautious handling of his cavalry, kept them off on the right. On the left, White's brigade was confronted by some 4,000 horsemen, of which 1,500 were Afghans. These made a wide sweep in an effort to turn the British flanks. Thackwell in person ordered Lieutenant Malcolm, commanding the Scinde Horse (only 243 strong), to bring his 'right shoulders forward and charge the Afghan cavalry'.[29] The 3rd, as well as the 9th Lancers, joined in this charge, as Pearman recounts in his narrative of what he saw of the battle:

About 10 a.m. I took a dispatch to the Colonel of the 10th Foot, with orders to advance and take the town in flank. They were about three miles from us. I found them all lying down waiting for orders. They told me that the 14th Light Dragoons had charged, led by Lieutenant-colonel Lockwood of the 3rd Light Dragoons. He was an acting Brigadier that day of the right cavalry brigade. As soon as I gave the dispatch to the Colonel of the 10th Foot, he looked at it and called out: 'Fall in, 10th, we've got something to do at last.' I turned to go back to my regiment, when I heard the Colonel give the order 'Forward, 10th!', and away they went in line, but I had not got a half mile when I heard the enemy's guns at them, and the sepoys were following up to their support when I looked back. I struck my horse into a canter as so many of the other regiments asked me questions. I could not tell them, but by the time I got back to my regiment, the firing was coming up the whole line.

In a very few minutes the round six- and nine-pound shot and shell was flying over our heads. Captain Draper of ours, every shot that went over his head made him duck down his head. Colonel White, who had seen the Peninsula fights, and been at Waterloo, said: 'Captain, it is no use ducking. If there is one for you, I think you will get it.' This made us laugh, but Draper was a nice little officer, and a perfect gentleman. He replied: 'I can't help it, Colonel.' Just at that moment a nine-pound shot struck the ground at the Colonel's horse's heels, but Colonel White did not move or look round. His brave old face never moved, with his white hair round it. He only said: 'Steady, men, steady! Make much of your horses, men.' I think there was not a man or an officer who knew Colonel White that did not love him: such a happy face, and so kind to all. But he could be severe if he liked.

Just at this time we were ordered to advance, covered by skirmishers, which we did, and closed up to the enemy. Some of our boys fell. But we were laying a trap for some of their artillery, who followed us back as we retired by alternate squadrons, covered by skirmishers. Their artillery followed us and unlimbered about a hundred and fifty yards from the cornfield where lay the 60th Rifles. As soon as they got the six guns to practice on us, we halted and showed a front and sounded 'Skirmishers in'. Then up got the 60th Rifles, and killed every man of that Troop. We then went and spiked the guns and left them.

The battle was now at its highest, and the air had become filled with shot, shell and smoke. Trumpets were sounding, drums beating, bugles sounding, colonels and other officers hollering, when all of a sudden came the order for the 3rd Light Dragoons to charge. I could see the 9th Lancers and the black cavalry doing the same. But we did not get much at them this time, as they made a quick movement back into their line. We got among some of their horse and killed a few. My horse ran against one of theirs and knocked him down. It hurt my leg very much as it struck his horse's shoulder. I put my sword into the man and went on with the rest. We came to a halt on the left of the town of Gujrat, when their guns began to give it us again hot.

But in a short time we advanced again at a trot. In front of us was a long hedge of prickly pear, a sort of cactus plant about five or six feet high. This plant grows very large in that country. The enemy's guns were behind this hedge, and it was very thick, but at it we went, and through it, the pricks sticking into man and horse. Just over this hedge, about forty yards on, was a large hole made for their cooks to put slush into, and my horse's forelegs went into this hole, and he turned completely over with me. I lay with my right leg on my carbine, and my horse lay on my right leg. I seized my pistol, for the enemy's foot were all over the place. I heard Tom Taylor say, 'Pearman's shot', but I knew better.

My comrade, William Makepiece, came back to me as the regiment halted about two hundred yards off. He said, 'Shake the damned reins and make him get up, Jack.' He kept cantering round me with his sword, and kept off the straggling foot of the enemy. At last my horse got up and let my leg loose. I found I was not hurt much. Makepiece said: 'Here is one of their horses out here,' and I made for it, but Captain John Sullivan came and said my horse was caught at the regiment, so off we went. I got on the rascal again. One of my reins was broken. I tied it together. It sounded 'Skirmishers to the front' and we changed our direction to the left. The men out skirmishing had some sharp work for about half an hour, when it sounded 'Skirmishers in', and back they came.

As the Sikhs in the centre gave way, Captain Delmar of the 9th Lancers saw our troops 'driving them before them like so many sheep.... The whole line pursued them, cutting them down right and left.... We at last came upon a number of their guns which they in the hurry of their flight had left.... [We] overtook numbers of their infantry who were running for their lives — every man of course was shot.... I never saw such butchery and murder! It is almost too horrible to commit to paper.... But besides all this *ground* shooting, there was an immense deal of *tree* shooting.... Every tree that was standing was well searched, and two or three Sikhs were found concealing in almost every tree we passed — this afforded great sport for our men, who were firing up at them, as at so many rooks.... Down they would come like a bird, head downward, and bleeding most profusely.'[30]

Gujrat was the first battle in either of the Sikh wars in which the cavalry had an opportunity for a sustained chase of a broken enemy. The regiments had received orders, before the battle began, 'not to draw rein until their horses drop in the pursuit'.[31] The whole cavalry division, perhaps 5,000 men, joined together north of Gujrat, to take part in it.

I could now see that the whole of the cavalry was to the front, as far as I could see right and left. It now seemed that the battle was drawing to a close, as we could see the enemy in full retreat. Lord Gough came down the front with his staff. His leg was bleeding a little below his knee. A piece of shell had struck him I afterwards heard. The old man said: 'Thank you, 3rd Light, a glorious victory, men!' As soon as he had been down the cavalry front, we got the order to advance in pursuing order. The whole of the regiments, six or seven thousand strong,[a] covered eight or ten miles of front, when in pursuing order three yards apart. We pursued the poor flying devils to the banks of the Indus river.

It was now nearly dark but the right division of the army was ordered to cross the river, which they did in the night, and followed the routed enemy as long as there were any left.

Some of the cavalry regiments covered up to seventeen miles that night. In spite of these efforts, most of the enemy's horse managed to get clean away, nor were the casualties in the other arms very great. The pursuit was not ordered, it seems, as soon as it might have been. 'The reason given', according to an officer of the Scinde Irregular Horse, 'was that Lord Gough thought Gujrat still occupied.'[32]

On the whole it seems likely that the British cavalry was more judiciously handled at Gujrat than in any of the battles of the two Sikh wars, with the exception of Aliwal.

My regiment with the remainder of the army returned to

[a] The figure is more like 5,000.

Gujrat where our tents were left, but we were too much worn out to pitch tents. We got something to eat from the cooks, and lay down for the rest of the night. I had been twenty hours in the saddle, and cannot say the miles we rode.

The total British casualties at Gujrat were 96 killed and 706 wounded. The cavalry lost only three men killed (of which two were from the Scinde Irregular Horse), and forty wounded. Fifty-three guns were taken and a number of colours.

The battle effectively ended the war. The Sikhs surrendered unconditionally. Dalhousie, on his own responsibility, for he could get no intelligible guidance from London, decided upon full annexation of the Punjab. Thereby he added an enormous frontier tract to the domains of the Company.

The next morning we were so stiff we could not do anything, and I was very sore from my fall, and my right leg was very much bruised. But we were to have a standing camp and live in clover, as the enemy was entirely cut up, and peace was to be settled at Lahore as soon as the Durbar could be held by the Governor-General, who had been sent to. We remained some weeks at Gujrat, until the enemy had been sent back and had had to surrender his guns and all arms of war to the Commander-in-Chief, Sir Hugh Gough.

* * *

We had very good times at Gujrat. In the afternoon after the battle of February 21st, 1849, myself, Privates Makepiece, Ike Stagg, William Penfold and one or two others went into the town, where were many more soldiers of other regiments, to look at the place. We came across an old money changer, and made him tell us where he had put his money, but he would not say, until we showed him our pistols, when he gave us a bag of gold, about one quart, with silver. Stagg put it on his shoulder, and we were marching off with our loot, when we were met by one of the officers belonging to our prize agents. He said: 'What have you got there, soldiers, in that bag?' So Stagg dropped it on the ground and said, 'Look, sir.' The officer marked a broad arrow on it and said: 'Bring it along,' but we walked off and left him to do what he liked with it. We heard no more about it. He could not tell to what regiment we belonged as we were in white shirts and draws and pugerrie cap.

We went down a street to the bazaar, where we saw a fine Arab horse tied down with head and heel ropes, with a pink mane and tail, and a white body: a beauty. Makepiece said, 'You can't ride him, Sergeant.' I said I could. The black syce or groom said, 'Nay, nay, sahib, nay puckerroe (steal),' but I got on his back for a ride, and the rascal ran away with me, but I managed to get him to our camp. Captains Draper and Ouvry of C and H Troops saw me ride him in, and said, 'Pearman, where did you get the Arab?' I told them: 'We found it on the edge of the jungle.' Ouvry said, 'What do you want for it?' I said, 'Two flasks of grog and a hundred rupees (£10).' After some time he gave us one flask of grog and the one hundred rupees, and I am sorry to say we spent the money in more grog, which did us much harm.

On February 24th, my birthday, I had been out mounted to reconnoitre, which we did when on picquet, when we saw a man with a two-bullock hackery, and two chests of rupees. Johnny Grady asked him where it came from. He said he was sent from the town, so we took it, and filled our holster pipes on the saddle, and collected some gunpowder that was laying about, left by the enemy in lumps when in retreat, and blew the rest up. The bullocks and the man went away.

We heard no more of him. This was the only way to get prize money, for the Company only gave us six months' *batta*: £3 16s. 0d. in all. We made what we could and did very well, that is if we had not spent it in a very foolish way, I mean drink, which takes away the reason. After a few days the Prize Agents had got all that was worth having, but nevertheless the division of the army that came down from Multan Fort had plenty of money, round their body, and the waist of their trowsers lined with gold, and braces lined up and over the shoulders, and although the 10th Foot and 32nd and 60th Regiments had been searched many times by the Prize Agents and their officers, still they had plenty of money. The men robbed one another when drunk very much, which continued some weeks even after the army had been removed to Meen Mear, the great parade ground and barracks at Lahore belonging to Ranjit Singh and about two miles from the city.

The 3rd Company of the 4th Battalion of Foot Artillery, Bengal Troop, had to bring down the treasure, and they buried a quantity of it near unto Lahore, and began to sell some. When it came to the General's ears and a search was made, a woman of the 14th Light Dragoons split counsel, and the 3rd Company of Artillery were all placed under arrest, officers and all, as all had a finger in the pie. The 14th Dragoons and some sepoys had to do duty over them for some time; but they never found the treasure, and I have no doubt it is there to this day, as we were taken away from Lahore and no one was left, and the men of the 3rd Company never split.

The 10th Regiment of Foot had the most money. Armourer Sergeant Williams of the 10th was supposed to have got the gold-hilted sword belonging to the Maharajah of Multan, set with diamonds. They searched for it, but never got it. They tried him for plunder, reduced him to a private soldier, and they tried him again and sentenced him to one hundred lashes which he, poor fellow, got every one of. The gold hilt and diamonds were thrown into a well at Lahore by a private. I knew the man well. He was afraid to keep it for fear of being flogged. So there they remain.

Poor Williams, after he was flogged, got an exchange into my regiment, the 3rd Light Dragoons. He gave £100 to a man named William Walker to change regiments, which they got done. Walker had a black wife and wanted to stay in the country. When we came to England, Williams was promoted to be Armourer Sergeant. He died at Exeter in Devonshire from the effects of drink. He always had plenty of money and spent it very freely with his comrades. He was well beliked by them. I fired over his grave, poor fellow. Many an officer has taken more in other ways and not got flogged. Our own Commander-in-Chief had many things given to him by Maharajah Gulab Singh, and I think, as they were our enemy, that was anything but right. The poor soldier must not take anything from the enemy.

After a short time the arms of the enemy were collected and sent away under an escort to Lahore. The rest of the army followed and we arrived at the old Sikh parade ground, Meen Mear, a fine flat place, which could hold 50,000 men in camp. At this place we were halted for some time.

General Gough left us and General Sir Charles Napier (see p. 137) took the command of the army. We were reviewed by him. After we had been drawn up in close column of squadrons, also the 14th Light Dragoons, General Napier said, '3rd Light Dragoons, I am proud to see you. You look a fine lot of young men, and the charge you made this day was similar to one I saw made by the regiment when at Salamanca. I say again, I am proud to have command of such men.' He then turned to the 14th Light Dragoons and said, '14th King's Own, I am proud to see you, for with the regiment I served in Picton's Light Brigade, and I see in front of me men with soldierly faces, broad chest, and long and powerful limbs, and if you had been properly handled on January 13th [the battle of Chilianwala], the disgrace that now hangs over the regiment could not have taken place.' At this, a young trumpeter, by name John Springate, about eighteen years old, rode up to the General and said: 'General, our Colonel is a coward.' General Napier said: 'Make that man a prisoner.' Which was done. After a little more talk we were dismissed to our tents. About an hour after this, as we sat in our tents we heard the report of a pistol, and in a few minutes came the report that Colonel King of the 14th Light Dragoons had blown out his brains, which was true. We were all very sorry that he did that, as we got no explanation [as to] what made the regiment retire in the way it did [at Chilianwala]. However John Springate was released from being a prisoner. He afterwards died at Ambala from the effects of drink.

In fact, Lieutenant-colonel King committed suicide in July 1850, not in 1849. In September of that year an anonymous trooper of the 14th wrote to the full Colonel of the regiment to vindicate King. He blamed his suicide upon three troopers, one of whom was Springate, whose 'false words' about their commanding officer preyed upon his mind.[33] Henry Havelock goes out of his way to show that King 'did all that the bravest of men could do to rally his panic-stricken men'[34] at Chilianwala, and it is generally agreed that at Gujrat he was far from cowardly.

Soon after this our division marched en route for Ambala, which place we reached on April 7th, 1849, our regiment taking the four right barracks, the 14th Light Dragoons the four left barracks. The centre barracks were left for the married sergeants, and the Sergeants' Mess Room and the temporary [?] stables were made also into married quarters and the canteens.

There were many widows and some young unmarried girls, fourteen years of age, who had to get married or go off pay. The widows had to go off pay at six months from the death of their husbands. So weddings went on merrily, as they are articles that would not keep, four or five a day. Some women in that country have several husbands before they are very old. I knew one that married her sixth husband in the regiment to which I belonged. She had been in several regiments. She came from the 75th Foot to us.

We remained at Ambala until September 1850, when we received orders to march. No one seemed to know to where we were going. At last, on September 20th,[a] we marched out of Ambala in the direction of the Sutlej river, having very easy marches. We enjoyed ourselves much on the way, never very tired, but we soon found we were destined for the Punjab, which we came to on December 6th. We crossed the river at Ferozepur, and then marched to Lahore, where we remained several days to refresh the horses. We then crossed the river Ravi into the Jullundur Doab. When we arrived at Jullundur we stayed three days with the 29th Foot, and played a cricket match. The non-commissioned officers gave a ball to us as our women and families were with us, and a splendid supper. Altogether it was a good turn out. But one of our married men, named George Friend, had a very narrow escape of his life, as he returned to camp at about 2

---

[a] Pearman's dates are here rather shaky. The regiment actually marched out of Ambala, in the course of periodical relief, for the newly formed cantonment at Sialkot, on October 22nd, 1850.

o'clock in the morning. About half a mile from the barracks he was caught in a lassoo by a Thug or Highway robber, but he put up his arm and the noose went over his head and arm, so he slipped it off.

The next day we again commenced our march towards Wazirabad and then on to Sialkot, an open jungle about twenty miles from Kashmir. Maharajah Gulab Singh came to see us, and we escorted him back to Kashmir, where we stayed some fourteen or fifteen days — only one squadron. I went with it, and a very fine country Kashmir is. We went back to Sialkot, and then began to clear the jungle away. The 24th Foot began to build barracks, and the native soldiers also. I had some good sport at this place with my gun, as there was plenty of wild fowl of all sorts, and such a quantity of small snakes, some to be found in the tents every morning.

In May 1850[a] we left Sialkot to go to Wazirabad, where there were some temporary barracks, which we were to occupy. About the end of May I was taken with a pain in my right side which got worse every day. One morning I had paraded the men for duty, and taken them back to the guard mounting, and had nearly got home, when I had to sit down I was so ill. After a short time I got to my room and lay down. Sergeant Cooper came and asked me what was the matter with me. I said I was very ill. He then sent me to the hospital, and I was seen by Mr Harding, a half-caste, then compounder for the regiment. He gave me some medicine. About 7 o'clock they all thought I was dying and sent again for Doctor Trousdel. At this time the men were standing round my cot, and several said I was dead, but I knew better. Micky Coughlin said, 'I shall send word to his Troop,' which he did, stating that I died at 7 o'clock. I did not think I was

[a] This, again, is a mistaken date. The 3rd left Sialkot on January 13th, 1851, and arrived at Wazirabad on the 17th.

dying. Although my sight was nearly gone, I could see the men as if I were looking through a thick fog. I felt no pain. My body felt all over as if the blood tingled, what people call having pins and needles. I felt quite helpless, but I felt two sharp pricks, one in each arm, and in a short time I opened my eyes and saw Doctor Trousdel leaning over me, with his gold lace coat, and gold epaulettes on. He had run from a Dress Mess dinner to attend to me. When I opened my eyes, he said 'Pearman, don't speak, don't move.' I again shut my eyes and lay quite quiet. He had bled me in both arms. He did not leave me for an hour. The next morning he came, and I was cupped, and had on my side many dozen leeches, and the day after that a blister over the whole of the sore places. I then remained for about twelve days. My side was a little better, but still very bad. The blister had nearly healed up when our head Doctor came, Dr Henderson by name, and they both examined me and came to the conclusion that to save my life my side must be opened and a small abscess cut away. They left me with this consolation.

The following day Doctor Trousdel asked me if I was willing to have my side opened as he said my life could not be saved without doing it, and perhaps not then. He was a Scotchman and a very plain-spoken man. Four days after this I was taken into a room at the end of the hospital, where Doctors Trousdel and D'Arcy performed the operation, which lasted about a quarter of an hour. I was then carried to a bed in the hospital with the other men. A silver pipe was in my side for some time, and served to carry off the discharge from the liver. When the pipe was taken out I had a seaton[a] put into my side underneath the place where the pipe was. The seaton was as large as a tobacco pipe, and this was kept

[a] *Seton:* A surgical thread or tape, etc., drawn through a fold of skin so as to maintain an opening for discharges.

General Sir Charles James Napier, aged 66, 1848 (*see p. 96*)

The Marquess of Dalhousie, Governor-General of India (*see p. 67*)

Sher Singh Atariwala (*see p. 67*)

(*Over*)

The charge of the 3rd Light Dragoons at the battle of Chilianwala

in for several months. Four months I was laid on my back, and eight places came through my skin, which had to be dressed by lifting me up on doubled up sheets.

When I was able to walk about I was allowed to leave the hospital for a walk in the morning and evening. As I got better I had to ride on an elephant, and at last on a camel, and then I had my horse to go out where I liked in the cantonments. They were very kind to me, and gave me every indulgence. I was eleven months from my duty.

* * *

About the time I got well the regiment got orders to return home to England. We commenced our march as soon as the cold season of 1852 set in, about the beginning of October.[a] We had our horses for about three weeks' march, and then they were taken away and sent to other regiments in the country. We stayed in tents several days until two flat-bottomed boats were got ready. These had to be towed along by two steam tugs. Into these boats we were packed like pigs at a market in a pen at night. On the boat I was in, twenty-five men had no room to lie down on the deck. No beds were allowed, as they would have been too hot. Sometimes in the day we were allowed to stretch our legs on the banks for an hour. We had made about two hundred miles in this way when the men grumbled so much that the officer in charge got a tent to hold thirty men, and this was put up every night for that number to lie in, as we did not travel at night. In this way we came eight hundred miles down the river Indus. Some days we had some sport, the officers shooting wild fowl, which we got our share of. We had a gun with a large mouth

---

[a] In fact the regiment left Wazirabad for Karachi, the appointed port of embarkation, via Multan, on November 20th, 1852.

which carried two or three pounds of shot. This was at the head of the boat on a swivel. When we came across a lot of water fowl, which are very numerous on the Indus, this gun was fired. Then the officers got into the boat and killed with small guns what was wounded, and got them into the boat. When we stopped at night we had a feast on these occasions.

We saw many sights on the Indus, some of the old places left by Alexander the Great. At one place there was a sort of raised platform of lime and earth beaten together, and in good preservation, said to be his Council table in his standing camp when on the Indus with his fleet.

At last we reached Karachi in the Bombay Presidency on February 3rd, 1853. About the end of the month we embarked in the ship *The Duke of Argyll*, an old wooden ship, very slow but very comfortable. She could stand rough weather without your being much tossed about. The regiment took three ships to bring us home. Our ship called at the Cape of Good Hope, where we took in more fresh water and stores, and I went on shore with others to change our rupees into English money; but at the Cape they were two pence less value to us than in India, but we had to lose it. In India a rupee is to the soldier 2s. 0½d., but at the Cape they would only give us 1s. 10½d. for the rupee, and in England 1s. 9½d. for the rupee, so they had us always. But it did not matter much, as soldiers are like sailors, when they come home what they don't spend in drink, the sharks steal that are always on the lookout at Chatham, the last place that God made, and that is why it is peopled with such a sort.

On our arrival in the Channel I was on watch, and when near Dover, and it was getting light, I saw what I thought was the stars going out, but the sailor on watch at the port cat head said it was the lamps being put out at Dover. I went to the ship's gangway and hollered down the hold to the men in their hammocks, 'There is Dover in sight!', when up they came in their shirts, and there was no getting them down again until they had seen Dover. At Dover we lay to, as we had to be medically examined before being allowed up the river. Then the Harbour Master allowed us to proceed to Gravesend, which place we reached on the night of Saturday, June 25th, 1853. We lay there all Sunday, as we were not allowed to land on Sunday. It was a fine day, but it seemed very cold to us. I thought I never was so cold, and with my cloak on. The pleasure steam boats from London came down with the roses of old England, dressed in white. They threw their pocket handkerchiefs to us, and some flowers, as the boats went round us, and kissed their hands, but they were not allowed very close.

The bumboats came alongside, and sold us things. Such a lot of roughs! If you let them have your money before you got hold of the article, you never got it at all. I gave a man in a boat a nearly new coat and trowsers made in Kashmir of camel hair, for a loaf of bread, and about one lb. of cheese, and most of that I gave the children, poor things.

On Monday, June 27th, 1853, the custom house officers came on board to see what we had got. They made a search of the ship and then the officers and then the men, and all our kits also; but we took them in after all, as we expected it would be so. The customs officers bought some of our cigars themselves. I sold one [of them] 300 chinsurah cigars at one penny each. They only cost me 1 rupee 12 annas, about 3s. 6d. in English money [for the whole 300]. By the time this was over it was 11 o'clock, and Gravesend was full of fathers, mothers, brothers, sisters, sweethearts and hundreds of girls and thieves. We commenced to land, and got on shore, but it was hard work to keep the men from the drink, so many people kept bringing it to them. At last we got into the train for Chatham, all standing — so many friends and all — as close as we could stand: women, girls and all. When we got to Chatham we were taken to the casemates for our quarters, and then left to ourselves to be robbed, for on that night several of the men lost their medals and money. We remained at Chatham about six weeks. There was a continual scene of drinking: from seventy, eighty or ninety prisoners to be taken before the Colonel every morning for being absent and drunk.

While at Chatham the regiment being nearly 700 men, the depot at Maidstone was opened to give volunteers to any of the light and heavy cavalry. The men that volunteered were to receive £1 10s. 0d. About 360 volunteered to the regiments going out to the Crimea.

We at last got the order to go to Exeter in Devonshire. I was sent with three others to Bath to get billets for the regiment which came by train. Many of the men had gone to other regiments to collect horses. The regiments at home and in Ireland gave us so many each, as they could spare, so as to give us a start. We got about 150 horses in this way. The remainder which we got were young ones which we trained ourselves. While at Exeter the Crimean War was declared, and the 8th Hussars came to Exeter, and we played them off to Plymouth to embark.

We now received orders to march to Manchester. While we were there the Scots Greys came and stayed a week with us and then embarked at Liverpool. At this time our duty was very hard, training recruits and young horses. We could not get them ready fast enough. I went to Burnley and had sixty old soldiers with me. We were drilling all day, and still we could not get enough — plenty of recruits, but we had to make soldiers of them in six weeks. Poor boys! They went out to

Turkey like lambs to be slaughtered, as they could not ride; but they had to go.

In March 1856, I had to go to Sandhurst College to assist to drill the Gentlemen Cadets, and soon after I got there, the Riding Master, Captain Ward, broke his leg, and left me in charge of the Riding School altogether. A lance-sergeant of the 9th Lancers, Matthews by name, came from Canterbury to help me. I worked very hard in the Riding School at Sandhurst, and was there promised a Staff appointment, but when the Crimean War was over, the Duke of Cambridge, the Commander-in-Chief, said there would not be any more staff appointments made, as there would be a reduction in the army of 20,000 men. When I heard this it made me very much dissatisfied with the army after the hard work I had. So I made up my mind to leave, if they would let me, which they did after a great deal of trouble, by my paying to them £5, after all my hard service.[a]

---

[a] For twelve years from 1817, the cost of buying a discharge, whatever a man's length of service, was fixed at £20. In 1829, it was, for the first time, graduated according to the years spent with the colours. Had Pearman served for 15 years (he had in fact served for only 13), he would have had a free discharge. After 16 years' service, a bonus of six months' pay was given, and so on, on an ascending scale.

I certify that Serjeant John Pearman during his service of 13½ yrs with the 3rd Light dragoons, bore an excellent Character, I consider him a sober, steady and honest Man, & worthy of any situation his abilities will allow him to fulfil.

*W. Unett Lieut Colonel
Commanding 3rd Light dragoons*

*Hounslow
February 16th 1857.*

Sergeant Pearman's certificate of discharge, signed by
Lieut.-col. Walter Unett, February 16th, 1857

118

CHAPTER IV

I LEFT the regiment in disgust in February 1857, and on March 16th I joined the Buckinghamshire Police at Aylesbury. On May 7th I was ordered to a station, and went out as groom and lockup keeper to Superintendent Bragg, at Steeple Claydon, where I remained until June 1859, when I was promoted to acting sergeant and sent to Long Crendon, Bucks.

In September of that year I was sent on detective duty to find the writer of a threatening letter sent to P.C. David Flinn, stationed at North Crawley, in which letter it was stated that the writer would shoot him and a magistrate named David Selby Lowndes of Bucks. I dressed ragged, and had a small parcel of writing paper to sell. Sometimes I begged. It was three weeks before I could get a clue, but in October I found that a gypsy by name Thomas Saunders was sleeping in a stable at the Swan public house at Sherrington, Bucks. With the assistance of the police constable at that place, I got the landlord to let me also sleep in the stable, by making him believe I was hard up. In the morning we both got up. It rained and was very cold. We went into the tap room and I called for a pint of beer, which we had together near the fire. We began to talk of various things, when I asked him if he could write me a letter to a comrade that had deserted his regiment, and was then at Buckingham. He said he would. We then both went to the Windsor Castle public house at Sherrington, near Newport Pagnell. The landlady

119

supplied me with the paper and ink, and some more beer and bread and cheese, which I paid her for. She had a baby in her arms which I wanted her to sell to me; but she was very indignant. I only did this so as to draw her attention to Saunders while he was writing the letter. I tore the paper in half sideways and gave her the half I did not want then and asked her to keep it for me as I should want to have another letter written; but really so that she might produce it as a witness that Saunders wrote the letter for me on the other half, when I should want her evidence. Then I put the letter in my pocket and went to Newport Pagnell to see Inspector Shepherd and the magistrate. It was bench day, and they made out a warrant for his apprehension. I took it to Flinn, police constable at North Crawley, for him to find Saunders and apprehend him, which he did that night at Bedford.

When Saunders saw me and found I was a police constable he opened his eyes and looked at me, and so did the landlady when she brought the half sheet of my paper and gave her evidence. Saunders was committed for trial and had to wait five months and some days before it came on, when he was sentenced to nine months more. A great number of people of North Crawley came to hear the trial, as I had lodged at several public houses, and told them many a soldier's tale of India and the campaigns I had been in. After the trial was over they made me go to the Bull Inn, Aylesbury and have dinner with them. They laughed at my wanting to buy the baby, and so did the Judge smile [*sic*].

After this I was made full sergeant. I was then stationed at Long Crendon. I went on several other cases as detective and was very successful. In January 1862 I was promoted to Second Class Inspector, and sent to take charge of Great Marlow, which place I became very fond of. It was a nice home and a good garden. In 1863 I went as a detective with

Sergeant Story to Stoke Goldington, where Lord Carrington had a farm burnt, and all the ricks. The young man that did it had enlisted for a soldier and gone to Tilbury Fort. He had been home on furlough. He was apprehended on our evidence by a warrant and brought to Aylesbury, where he was tried and got fifteen years' transportation. I got a £5 reward.

After this I was promoted to First Class Inspector in January 1864, and sent to take charge of the men employed at Eton College and the Street, and here I remained until I tendered my resignation to the Chief Constable, being 62½ years of age. At the October Quarter Sessions of 1881, I was granted a pension from the superannuation fund, of £69 6s. 8d. per year. I was 17 years and 9 months stationed at Eton College, and on my retirement was presented with a testimonial in vellum, with the words: 'To John Pearman of Eton. We the inhabitants of Eton desire to convey to you on your retirement as Inspector of Police for the past 17 years, our appreciation of the faithful manner you fulfilled that office, and beg your acceptance of the accompanying purse of money. That your future may be blessed with all the good this world can afford is the sincere wish of the subscribers.'

Thus ended my public service of forty years in uniform. But I must confess if I had my time to see again, it would not be passed in the same way.

CHAPTER V

Nowhere in his 'memoirs' does Pearman mention in what year he married. It was probably soon after his return to England in 1853, when he was thirty-four years old. His wife's maiden name was Elizabeth Collins, and she came from Berkshire. She was much younger than her husband, bore him eleven children, of whom eight survived infancy, and outlived him by several years.

What is marriage [he asks] but a life of trouble and care, and in most cases of the poor, a great deal of poverty? My own married life has been a life of much care. I have always been a very careful man, never making any waste of money or anything else, by which means I was able to save a little money to meet any trouble in old age.

The early part of my married life was, I suppose, much the same as other people's: sometimes a few sharp and hot words with the wife, but soon over, mine being a very hot temper and my wife being of a very different disposition from mine. On the whole we got on as well as most people. I would always be master of the home, and I spent the money, as I found my wife was not up to the mark in laying out money to the best advantage. But this never led to words. These were always about the children. A wife can be too much of a mother and indulge the children in every folly. I must say this was the case with my wife. She is a most hard-working woman and on the whole a careful woman. But she has a very bad fault—that is ingratitude. She always was ungrateful, thinking man had nothing else to think of but her. It did not matter what you gave her in the way of money, she never was thankful for it. I never spent a shilling from the home, but that she never took into account. Perhaps had I been a man otherwise, I might have been better thought of, as then she would have had to work to bring something to help to maintain the children. But I know she had enough to do to keep the house and children straight, and this she did much to her great credit, for the children were always clean and fit to be seen. I must do her justice, the children were taught no bad ways, nor did they see any.

I used to save some money every year so as to give them a day's outing—sometimes two days—and go to Sandhurst. This gave me more pleasure than anything I ever had. About halfway to Sandhurst we used to stop on the side of the road, put the nose bag on the horse for him to feed, and then take out the children and give them cake, wine and some other kind of food, and when all had been satisfied, we went on our journey. This we did for many years, and it lives in my mind's eye. I can even enjoy the sight now when I think of it, and picture their happy young faces. That I think is the real bliss of a married life. But no affection ought to make us blind to the faults of the children, or the mother. We may accept them as part and parcel of the beloved, but we ought not to ignore them or call them good. The children loved beyond reason is a lasting fault of the parent. We must do our duty in order to love them. Such love is passionless. Duty gives neither kisses nor caresses.

I have always tried to do my duty to my God without any show of religion, and my wife also without any show of any kind. Mine was not a boyish love; it was the love of a man to do my duty and take care of her. When I took her from her father's home, I swore to God to do my best to maintain her in comfort, and this I have done up to now, and with the help of God I will continue to do so. If it please God to take me first, all I have in this world or coming to me is hers and for her own disposal. I am not afraid that she will go wrong with it, although I know my wife never had much affection for me, but I swore before God to do my best by her, and I will try to do so until my life ends. When I married her I was aware of the difference of our ages, and she knew the same, and it should not make any difference as to our duty to each other.

I was a man that could not make away much money if I had the chance; but with eight children, an Inspector of County Police has not much to spare.

> Soon after the birth of his first child, a daughter called Rose, Pearman changed his station (presumably within Buckinghamshire),

as a constable, and my second child, John, was born, and now more want of money! But I worked hard, and was rewarded with promotion and more money and another change of station—to Great Marlow—with the rank of inspector. I continued to work hard and was often sent out on detective duty. I was very successful, and got another step in promotion when my third child Elizabeth was born, and another change of station—to Eton College, with the rank of First Class Inspector. Here I remained until I left the Police Force. I must say I was very much better off at Eton as my pay was better and my duty much lighter. I was nearly my own master, and the people were a sort of persons that wanted but little looking after. My worst duty was seeing to the College students, but I did not make a trouble of that. The Head Masters seldom said much, if things were alright. They knew what the students were: they had been at College themselves as boys.

Taking things as a whole I was very comfortable at Eton, but I had many trials as a father. In the year 1866 my children took gastric fever, and Arthur, the baby, was nearly dying, and I lay by the side of his cradle all my spare time, by day and night for seventeen days, expecting each to be his last.

We got over all that and paid a good sum to Dr Gooch. All went well until the end of August 1867, when one morning after breakfast John could not stand, and was very ill. In a little time after, Lizzie was the same. I went to Dr Gooch and when he came he said they had got the scarlet fever. In a few days more Arthur was also taken with it. Rose was poorly but not ill. My wife had a baby, 4 months old, and was ill, and not able to give the baby the breast. It was weaned at this time. The students were at home on their holidays and would return on September 18th, 19th and 20th. I lived near the College, in fact almost in it. Dr Balston was the Head Master [see p. 133]. He sent for me and said he should like me and my family to leave the College until we were all well, as he could not have the students back while such a bad case of fever was in the College. He said the College would pay any extra expence I might be put to.

Dr Gooch and Dr Pearle both said I must not move them but a few miles, as the children could not stand a journey of long distance. Dr Balston said I could go to the sea side, but the Doctors said I must not be on the road over an hour. Now here was a trial for a man. To move my wife and children almost said death to some of them, but again I thought of the tradespeople of Eton. It had been the long holiday, and people having no work had become short of money. So I made up my mind to do my best to get the wife and children to some place. For three days I drove all round the place for miles. William Harris went with me. I had his pony and cart. No one cared to take me in, but at last a Mr Cam, a nice man, and his wife, said they would take their chance and take us in, as they were in want of money. He was the landlord of a public house at Winkfield, Berks. I then felt a little more lighthearted and drove home.

Now came another fix. I could not get a conveyance to take us. They said no one would ride in it after us. Mr F. Bunce of the Turk's Head, Eton, saw how I was fixed. When me and Harris put the pony into his stable and went to the bar to have some gin, he said 'What is the matter, Mr Pearman?' I told him the whole and he acted a man. He said 'I am not a rich man, but you can take my brougham for your wife and children, and if people won't ride in it after, I will burn it, and my van shall take what other things you want.' I could not thank him enough. But he said 'No thanks. I may want the same or something, of someone some day. Now sit down a bit and then let me know at what time you will want it.' It was arranged that I should start at 10 the next morning, and true to time he was at my gate with the closed trap and his van. I got my wife in with the baby, and the two year old one on her lap. John I put into a blanket in the corner by his mother. I then got Lizzie into another blanket and put her in with her sister Rose, who was well, to hold her on the seat. I got on the box with the driver. Prior to this I had put my bedding into the van for their use at Winkfield.

We started at 10 a.m. and had got through Windsor to the foot of High Standing Hill when my wife tapped on the fly's window. We stopped. John was taken worse. I looked at him and he, poor boy, was like death. The motion of the fly had made him feel sick. I rolled the blanket round him and took him out, when he was very sick. At this time a gentleman came up on horseback and said 'Do you know what's the matter with that boy?' I didn't answer him as the boy was vomiting. He said 'He has the scarlet fever.' I replied 'I know that.' He then looked in the fly and said 'Inspector,' (I had my uniform on) 'they have all got the fever. Where are you taking them to?' I replied 'Unto Winkfield.' He said 'No. That you shan't.' I replied 'I shall', and put my son in the fly again, and was about to get on the seat myself when he said 'What is your name? I am the doctor of Winkfield and must know.' He gave me his name when I showed him the paper for their removal signed by Drs Gooch, Pearle and Ellison, and told him to go and see the Head Master of Eton College, which he did. When he came back he was in a better temper. I supposed the Head Master had tipped him, for when he called on me at the public house I was staying at, he said it was alright, and I could get anything I might want at his surgery. I remained at Winkfield until November 5th when I returned with my family again to Eton, and thank God they continued to do well and again got strong.

* * *

The last hundred or so pages of Pearman's 'memoirs' are filled to a large extent with his comments upon the world in which he found himself.

My nature [he writes] was not to take pleasure, but to watch the ways and doings of mankind, and to learn if possible what man has to live for. I must be very thankful. I have never been out of employment or without a shilling. I have been very lucky and had good health.

In spite of such occasional expressions of gratitude, the greater part of his reflections betrays a deep bitterness about the existing order and the injustices of society.

What is a soldier? [he asks.] A man forced down under the brutalising machine of military life, which presses out nature from the very veins and bones of its victims, and shapes from the warm living flesh a puppet, a tool, a thing, a creature without eyes or ears or sense or will of its own. A plaything for death, a missile in the merciless hand of the state for pomp and vainglory.[a]

In another passage he gives it as his

sincere impression that man was not made to slaughter his fellow man, for any other man or the State, although he may have engaged himself as an hired assassin.

Yet he admits that that part of his life which he spent soldiering in India

was the most worth living, for although we oftimes had to face death in the worst form, there is a pleasure in that, for it places the great man and the poor on a footing. I have oftimes put my foot on a dead officer as we put his body under ground, and said to myself 'Where is your rank now?' Then Mr Officer was not the same *tyrant* in India that he was in England. Dead men tell no tales. They know that out there.

At the time I am speaking of, India was to the white man a free country. We could go where we liked. No trespass out there, and John Company behaved well to us, shared some of the plunder with us soldiers, I mean in prize money. Not so the Queen's Government. Then John Company did not make us work, found us plenty of servants, plenty of grog and good

[a] This reads like, and may well be, a quotation from a contemporary 'radical' publication.

Captain Walter Unett, as Lieutenant-colonel, 3rd Light Dragoons, *c.* 1855

Shabracque carried by Captain Unett's charger at the battles of Sobraon and Chilianwala

Sketch made by Captain Unett, showing the mêlée resulting from his squadron's charge at Chilianwala. He himself is depicted (*centre*) about to receive a sword wound, the effects of which upon his jacket are seen in the illustration opposite

Stable jacket worn by Captain Unett at Chilianwala, showing the
sword cut across the shoulder, and the marks (*bottom right*) of the
spear thrust in the side (*see p.* 91)

John Pearman in old age

Pearman's Punjab Campaign Medal, 1848–9

living. If they were thieves, and stole the country, I must say
they gave some of it to the blood hounds who hunted down
the rightful owners (i.e. the soldiers). Well with all the faults
of a military life, there is more to live for than the poor man
who in England is a free paid slave.

I cannot say much for the policeman's life. He must be a
special man, and look after other men's faults, and shut his
eyes to all his virtues. I must say I did very well in the police
force.

Against the 'establishment' in general and organized
religion in particular, Pearman is rancorous.

Look [he writes] at the difference of the start in life. Our
Queen [whom elsewhere he refers to sarcastically as 'the
goddess Victoria'] had a noble start. Compare that with the
gutter children of the earth, and look at their start. They
surely have nothing to thank God for.

I know we must have rulers, but not as they now live, in
luxury and riot.

The rich break the laws they have made for their own ends,
and the lawyer will drag them out of their own dirt for the
golden calf — money.

Look at the pride of the Church — the Bishop must have his
coach to go to church on Sunday. But we must highly respect
the founders of many religions — and one in particular — Jesus
of Nazareth. He paid the penalty of the law of his day, as
many have done since, in England.

Man attends his worship in church, but in his race for
wealth he forgets both God and Church, and only keeps the
semblance.

The Archbishop and the Clergy send up prayers for our
armies in the field. Oh, what cant!

What we want is righteousness, not religion, but landlords

I   129

must have their rent, no matter what the value of the crop. This is the rub. Money is the God of the great.

As a half-breed Welshman, I must hate the English as the Irish hate them, and I have long time wished that something would turn up with England and America so that England might get a sound beating by them. The Irish would then be able to get back their own country again.

The best love we have for each other is for our own advantage. For instance when we find a part of the world that would be of use and a profit to us, we at once covet the same. We wish to make Christians, i.e. to *covet* their country. Our first step: send out six or eight missionaries, men with many faces but one head. They meddle with the ways and the views that God has given them in his omnipotence. But the Christian does not consider that he has given them the right way of thought. Well, to bring about this our next step is to send a few soldiers. They will soon show the way to become Christians. The next step is: 'You must pay for the loss you have put us to by being so stubborn as not to accept our views of religion.' Now comes the grand step: annexation of their country, and in a short time we send them a bishop and all his host, and they must pay for that likewise. Oh, John Bull, you are a great rogue!

I once said to an Indian black man, 'Why do you trust and put such faith in the water of the Ganges?' He replied, 'I act as I was taught. You do the same. I could ask you, why do you put such faith in Jesus? You would say I was taught to do so.' But he enlightened me on one thing that I could not deny. He said, 'You have a trinity in unity, the Father, Son and Holy Ghost. Now' he said, 'I can tell you in that you are right. You have the Gun, Sword and the Bayonet in unity, and in them you put your trust, and you should do so, for they have made your nation great, and brought you all you have.' Now, when I see a gun, I take off my hat to the National Idol and say 'Salaam'.

*　　*　　*

And so, in much the same vein, Pearman rambles on, page after page, sometimes amusingly, more often in increasingly sour disillusionment. Gradually and almost imperceptibly his firm, neat handwriting loses its trim steadiness, as he slips, growling, into old age.

After retiring from the police force there remained to him a further twenty-seven years of life. He died on November 28th, 1908, at the advanced age of eighty-nine, almost certainly the last survivor of the battle of Aliwal, in which he had fought with Alexander's Bengal Horse Artillery sixty-two years before.

BIOGRAPHICAL NOTES

Brevet Lieutenant-colonel (later General Sir) James ALEXANDER, K.C.B. (1802–88) (see p. 47), was a product of Addiscombe, the H.E.I.C.'s college; 2nd lieut. Bengal Artillery, 1820; colonel, 1854; col. commandant, R.A., 1872. He served in the Afghan War of 1842, and the Gwalior campaign of 1843.

The Reverend Edward BALSTON, D.D., M.A. (1817–91) (see p. 125), was educated at Eton and at King's College, Cambridge. He was an assistant master at Eton from 1840 to 1860, and a fellow from 1860. In 1862 he succeeded to the headmastership, which he resigned in 1867. He was archdeacon of Derby from 1873 to just before his death. There is a recumbent figure of him in Eton College Chapel.

Brigadier-general Charles Robert CURETON, C.B. (1789–1848) (see p. 39), was the son of a Shropshire squire. He obtained a commission in the local Militia in 1806. His extravagant habits soon forced him to flee from his creditors. For this purpose he left his uniform on a beach to simulate accidental drowning and went off to London in the disguise of a sailor. There he enlisted as a private in the 14th Light Dragoons, under the *nom de guerre* of Robert Taylor. He speedily became a sergeant, and went through the Peninsular War with distinction, being thrice wounded. In 1813 he was recognized by Lord Fitzroy Somerset (later Lord Raglan), one of Wellington's staff officers, 'who had known him at home',[35] and before long he was given an infantry ensigncy without purchase. In 1819 he entered the 16th Lancers. He served in the first Afghan War, and commanded a cavalry brigade in the Gwalior campaign. He was killed at Ramnagar (see p. 75).

James A. B. Ramsay, 10th Earl and 1st Marquess of DALHOUSIE (1812–1860) (see p. 67), was the youngest son of the 9th Earl, who had been Commander-in-Chief in India from 1829 to 1832. Lords Canning and Elgin were his contemporaries at Harrow. Each of them held the governor-generalship of India in succession after him. In 1845 he became President of the Board of Trade, and two years later was appointed governor-general. He was then 36, and the youngest man who had ever held the appointment. At the end of the second Sikh War he was created a marquess. The construction by private enterprise, under direct government control, of the Indian railway system, was started by him. This, and the introduction of the telegraphs were among his outstanding personal contributions to the modernizing of the sub-continent.

In 1852, after the second Burmese War, he annexed Lower Burma. In the eight years of his rule, Dalhousie was responsible for the annexation of a number of native states, including Nagpur and Jhansi. In 1856 he was ordered to annex Oudh, a measure which was partially responsible for the Indian Mutiny which broke out in the year following his return to Britain. He died from overwork in his 49th year.

Major-general Sir Robert Henry Dick, k.c.b. (1785?–1846) (see p. 52), was the son of a poor Scottish doctor who made a fortune as a surgeon in the service of the East India Company. First commissioned in 1800, he was wounded at Maida in 1806, and served throughout the Peninsular War in the Black Watch. He was again wounded at Quatre Bras, but was nevertheless present in command of his regiment at Waterloo, where he particularly distinguished himself. In 1838, as major-general, he was given command of the centre division of the Madras Army. From this he was transferred to the Bengal Army in 1842. He was killed at the head of his Division at Sobraon (see p. 54).

Lieutenant-general Sir Walter Raleigh Gilbert, g.c.b. (1785–1853) (see p. 53), obtained in 1800 a Bengal infantry cadetship. He served in the 15th Bengal Native Infantry for ten years, taking part in Lord Lake's campaigns. In 1824 he became lieutenant-colonel of the 39th, and in 1832 colonel of the 35th Bengal Native Infantry. He was promoted major-general in 1841 and lieutenant-general ten years later. In the first Sikh War, at Mudki, Ferozeshah and Sobraon, and, in the second Sikh War, at Chilianwala and Gujrat (see pp. 84 and 98), he commanded an infantry division. In 1850 he was appointed a provisional member of the Council of India, and in 1851 he was created a baronet. Gilbert's reputation on the Indian turf and as a sportsman was considerable.

Field-marshal Sir Hugh (later 1st Viscount) Gough (1779–1869) (see p. 19) came of an old Limerick family. At 15 he was adjutant of an infantry regiment. He served in South Africa and the West Indies

(1795–1803), and throughout the Peninsular War. He commanded the 87th Foot (later the Royal Irish Fusiliers) at Talavera in 1809, where he was gravely wounded. At Wellington's request he was the first British officer ever to receive brevet promotion (to lieutenant-colonel) for service in action at the head of a regiment. At Barossa in 1811 he led the 87th Foot and part of the 1st Guards with extreme bravery. Later the same year he defended Tarifa, where the French commander fell mortally wounded at the portcullis which closed a breach in the walls, and gave up his sword to Gough through the bars. He was in action at Vitoria, and again severely wounded at the Nivelle. Knighted in 1815, he became major-general in 1830. Seven years later he obtained command of the Mysore division of the Madras army. In 1841 he was promoted to lieutenant-general on the same day as Henry Hardinge (see below). In 1841–2 he held the chief command in the China War which ended in the peace of Nanking. In 1843 he was appointed Commander-in-Chief, India, at the age of 64. He commanded the army in the successful 48-hour Gwalior campaign that same year.

After the first Sikh War he was created Baron Gough of Ching-keang-foo in China, Maharajpore and the Sutlej in the East Indies. After the second Sikh War he returned home to be made a viscount and receive a pension of £2,000 a year. He was promoted to full general in 1854, and became, on the death of Lord Raglan, in 1855, Colonel of the Royal Horse Guards. In 1857 he was made the first Knight of St Patrick not holding an Irish peerage, and in 1862 a field-marshal. Seven years later he died in his ninetieth year.

Gough was a forceful soldier, famed for his courage and determination, if not for his brilliance as a general. His noble presence and chivalry made him intensely popular with his troops, though he was at times prodigal with their lives. He is believed to have commanded in more general actions in the nineteenth century than any other British officer except Wellington.

An anonymous jingle referring to the period of the second Sikh War neatly presents a contemporary view of Gough:

> Sabres drawn and bayonets fixed,
> Fight where fought Alexander;
> Oh Paddy Gough's a cross betwixt
> A bulldog and a salamander.

Field-marshal Sir Henry (later 1st Viscount) HARDINGE (1785–1856) (see p. 32) was a grandson of the distinguished poet, Latin scholar and clerk to the House of Commons, Nicholas Hardinge (1699–1758).

He was one of the earliest pupils of the Royal Military College when it was still at High Wycombe. At 14 he was bought an ensigncy in an infantry corps. He joined Arthur Wellesley as a staff officer, and was wounded at Vimeiro (1808). He served through the retreat to Corunna and was with Moore at his death. From 1811 he served on Marshal Beresford's staff with the Portuguese army, and received a colonelcy without purchase. He commanded a Portuguese brigade at the storming of Palais, near Bayonne, in 1814. The same year he became 'captain and lieutenant-colonel' in the 1st Guards (the Grenadiers), with which regiment he remained till 1827. In the Netherlands campaign of 1815, Hardinge, whose superior intelligence and capacity for hard work were early appreciated by Wellington, was military commissioner at Blücher's headquarters. He lost his left hand at Ligny.

Hardinge was elected a Tory Member of Parliament in 1820, and became, first, secretary at war (1828–30), and then, for a short time, Irish secretary in Wellington's ministry. This post he held again in 1834–5. He was for a second time secretary at war, under Peel, from 1841 to 1844.

In the latter year he succeeded his brother-in-law, Lord Ellenborough, as Governor-General of India. Being present at some of the battles of the first Sikh War, he waived his right to command in the field, and served as Gough's second-in-command. At Ferozeshah, however, he momentarily reasserted his civil power to restrain the Commander-in-Chief from attacking, until the Ferozepur garrison had joined him.

After the war he was created Viscount Hardinge of Lahore, and granted a pension of £3,000 a year. He returned to England in 1847, first to become Master-General of the Ordnance, and then to succeed Wellington as Commander-in-Chief. In this post he remained till the end of the Crimean War, for the military unpreparedness for which, public opinion rather unfairly blamed him. He was promoted to field-marshal in 1855 and died, in his 72nd year, in 1856.

Lieutenant-colonel William HAVELOCK (1793–1848) (see p. 62) was the eldest brother of Sir Henry Havelock of Mutiny fame. He joined the 43rd Foot as ensign in 1810. He acquired renown at the age of 20 when he inspired a Spanish force to defeat the French at Vera in 1813. He there took at one bound a formidable *abattis* which had checked the Spaniards. From that day on he was known as 'el chico blanco' (the fair boy), the name with which the Spanish soldiers cheered on their blond leader. He became captain in the 32nd Foot in 1818, and exchanged to the 4th Light Dragoons in 1821. In 1841 he became second lieutenant-colonel of the 14th Light Dragoons, succeeding to the command in 1845. He was killed leading his regiment at Ramnagar (see p. 75).

Lieutenant-general Sir John Bennet HEARSEY (1793–1865) (see p. 100) was the son of an officer of Bengal native cavalry. In 1807 he was given a cavalry cadetship. Soon afterwards he joined the 8th Native Cavalry. He served with distinction in numerous Indian campaigns, and was in command of the Presidency, or Calcutta, district as a major-general when the Indian Mutiny broke out in 1857. He remained in this post, as a most experienced adviser to Lord Canning, the Governor-General, until 1861.

Colonel Sir George Henry LOCKWOOD, K.C.B. (1804–84) (see p. 65), cornet, 3rd Light Dragoons, 1825; lieutenant-colonel, 1846. He had command of the regiment throughout the first Afghan War, 1842. At the battle of Gujrat (see p. 100), he commanded a brigade. From 1872 till his death he was Colonel of the 3rd.

General Sir Charles James NAPIER, G.C.B. (1782–1853) (see p. 96), was one of the most brilliant, complicated and fascinating members of a family of illustrious soldiers and sailors. His first commission was dated 1794. He made his mark under Moore in the Corunna campaign of 1808, was wounded, taken prisoner and later exchanged. At the Coa and Busaco under Wellington he again distinguished himself. In 1839, during the Chartist riots, he was given command of the Northern District of England, as a major-general. In 1841 he was sent to India, where, at the age of 60, he became famous as the conqueror of Sind. 'We have no right to seize Sind,' he wrote, 'yet we shall do so, and a very advantageous, useful, humane piece of rascality it will be.' After the lightning and militarily spectacular campaign was over, *Punch* represented Napier as reporting it in a single-word telegram (an impossibility in Sind at that date!): 'Peccavi' ('I have sinned'). In 1847 he resigned the government of Sind. His *Life and Opinions*, written in 1857 by his brother Sir William, the historian of the Peninsular War, is a neglected masterpiece. Napier was an ardent military reformer. Lord Wolseley called him the real soldier's friend of the nineteenth century.

Lieutenant-general Sir Harry SMITH, bart., G.C.B. (1787–1860) (see p. 34), was the son of a surgeon. At 18 he was commissioned in the 95th Foot (later the Rifle Brigade). He served in the Corunna campaign of 1808, and throughout the Peninsular War. In 1812, two days after the storming of Badajoz, two beautiful Spanish girls, who had been maltreated by the soldiery, claimed Smith's protection. The younger of the two, Juana Maria de los Dolores de Leon, aged only 14, became his wife. She accompanied him on all his subsequent travels and campaigns, and was a well-known figure in London society for some years.

Smith was assistant quartermaster-general of the 6th Division at Waterloo. In 1834, on the outbreak of the Kaffir War, he became commandant of the forces in Cape Colony. His famous ride from Cape Town to Graham's Town — 700 miles in six days — is rightly celebrated as an almost unequalled feat of horsemanship.

In 1840, Smith, promoted to brevet colonel, was appointed adjutant-general of the 'Queen's Army' in India. As such he took part in the short Gwalior campaign of 1843. At the beginning of the first Sikh War he was given command of a division. After his brilliant victory at Aliwal (see p. 41) he was made a baronet.

From 1847 to 1852 he was Governor of the Cape of Good Hope. At Boomplaatz in 1848 he defeated the Boers, and in 1850 fought some skilful engagements against the Kaffirs. Ladysmith in Natal is called after his wife.

Lieutenant-general Sir John Rowland SMYTH, K.C.B. (1806?–73) (see p. 41), cornet, 16th Lancers, 1821; major, 1842; commanded the regiment from 1847 to 1855; present at Maharajpur (Gwalior campaign), and severely wounded at Aliwal, where he led the right wing of the 16th. His sister, 'the beautiful Penelope Smyth', married the Prince of Capua, son of Francis I, King of the Two Sicilies, brother of King 'Bomba'. The Prince's family opposed the marriage. Consequently, so as to make certain of it, the couple were married twice in Italy, once at Gretna, and finally by banns, after a special licence had been refused, at St George's, Hanover Square. Sir 'Jacky' Smyth was an Irishman. He commanded the centre division of the Madras army, as a major-general, from 1865 to 1870. He was Colonel of the 6th Dragoon Guards from 1868 to 1873. In 1870 he was made lieutenant-general.

Lieutenant-general Sir Joseph THACKWELL, G.C.B. (1781–1859) (see p. 29), was the son of a Worcestershire squire. At 17 he was commissioned as a cornet of fencible cavalry. In 1800 he joined the 15th Light Dragoons (later Hussars), and remained with that regiment for thirty-two years. He served in the Peninsular War (Corunna, Vitoria, Orthes, Tarbes, Pamplona and Toulouse) and at Waterloo, where he lost his left arm. He obtained command of the 15th in 1820 and retained it for twelve years.

In the first Afghan War and the Gwalior campaign he commanded all the cavalry. At the start of the second Sikh War he had command of a division, but succeeded Cureton as cavalry commander after Ramnagar (see p. 78). In 1849 he became Colonel of the 16th Lancers. In 1854 he was appointed inspector-general of cavalry, and died, aged 78, five years later.

Thackwell's *Military Memoirs,* edited by Colonel H. C. Wylly in 1908, are an important source for the first Afghan and the second Sikh Wars. His son wrote a history of the second Sikh War.

Lieutenant-general Sir Michael WHITE, K.C.B. (1791–1868) (see p. 49), was the son of a major in the 27th Light Dragoons. He was commissioned in the 24th Light Dragoons in 1804, and became a captain in 1815. He served in the Mahratta war, at the siege of Bhurtpore and in the first Afghan War, first in the 24th, next in the 11th and finally, from 1839, in the 3rd Light Dragoons. In December of that year he became lieutenant-colonel in the regiment, and remained such until his promotion to major-general in 1854. For much of that time he acted as a brigade commander. He was Colonel of the 7th Dragoon Guards for the last ten years of his life.

Lieutenant-colonel John William YERBURY (1804–58) (see p. 80) commanded the 3rd Light Dragoons throughout the second Sikh War, although he did not become a substantive lieutenant-colonel till June 7th, 1849. He seems to have spent the whole of his career in the regiment, until he sold out in 1854. The date of his first commission was 1827.

NOTES ON SOURCES

1. Spear, P. (Smith, V. A.), *The Oxford History of India*, Part III, 1964 edn., 612.

2. Lawrence, Sir Henry, *Essays, Military and Political*, 1859, 262–3.

3. Gordon, Sir J. J. H., *The Sikhs*, 1904, 143.

4. Fortescue, The Hon. J. W., *A History of the British Army*, XII, 1927, 368.

5. Maude, Lieut.-col. F. N., *Cavalry: its Past and Future*, 1903, 181.

6. Sir H. Smith to Sir J. Kempt, Feb. 24th, 1846: Smith, G. C. M. (ed.), *The Autobiography of Lieut.-gen. Sir Harry Smith*, 1902, II, 194.

7. Stubbs, Maj.-gen. F. W., *History of the Bengal Artillery*, 1895, III, 145.

8. Sir J. Thackwell's letter home, Mar. 26th, 1846, and Sir H. Smith to Sir J. Thackwell (n.d. 1850s?): Wylly, Col. H. C. (ed.), *The Military Memoirs of Lieut.-gen. Sir Joseph Thackwell*, 1908, 213–4.

9. Gough's Dispatch, Nov. 23rd, 1848: Thackwell, E. J. [son and A.D.C. to Sir Joseph], *Narrative of the Second Seikh War in 1848–49*, 1851, 287.

10. Gough to his son, Mar. 18th, 1849: Rait, R. S., *The Life and Campaigns of Hugh, 1st Visc. Gough, Field-Marshal*, 1903, II, 186–7.

11. Memo. by H. Havelock, 1849: Marsham, J. C., *Memoirs of Sir H. Havelock*, 1860, 178.

12. Capt. R. P. Apthorp to Col. H. B. Hamilton, Feb. 14th, 1899: Hamilton, H. B., *Historical Record of the 14th (King's) Hussars*, 1901, 571; Marshman, J. C., *Memoirs of Sir H. Havelock*, 1860, 178.

13. Gough to Lord Fitzroy Somerset, Nov. 26th, 1848: Rait, R. S., *Life of Gough*, 1903, II, 189.

Source Notes

14. H. Havelock to Col. Birch, Dec. 7th, 1848: Marshman, J. C., *Memoirs of Sir H. Havelock*, 1860, 176.

15. Apthorp: Hamilton, H. B., *14th Hussars*, 1901, 570.

16. Marshman, J. C., *Memoirs of Sir H. Havelock*, 1860, 175.

17. Gough's diary, Jan. 13th, 1849: Gough, Gen. Sir C., and Innes, A. D., *The Sikhs and the Sikh Wars*, 1897, 293.

18. Forrest, G. W., *Life of F.M. Sir Neville Chamberlain*, 1909, 210.

19. Dalhousie to Duke of Wellington, Jan. 22nd, 1849: Lee-Warner, Sir W., *The Marquess of Dalhousie*, 1904, I, 207.

20. Thompson, Gen. C. W., and Chetwynd, Visc., 'The 14th Light Dragoons at Chilianwala', *Journal of Royal United Service Institution*, XXXIX (Oct. 1895), 1021.

21. Unett to his father, Jan. 15th, 1849: *Walter Unett Papers* (kindly lent to me by their owner, Lieut.-col. W. H. Unett).

22. See, for example, Gough and Innes, *The Sikhs and the Sikh Wars*, 1897, 294.

23. Lieut. MacQueen's account: Wylly, *Thackwell*, 1908, 294.

24. Unett's account: Wylly, *Thackwell*, 1908, 293.

25. Rait, *Gough*, 1903, II, 238.

26. Fortescue, *History of British Army*, XII, 1927, 457.

27. Quoted in Rait, *Gough*, 1903, II, 270.

28. Rait, *Gough*, 1903, II, 274.

29. Malcolm to Capt. Pratt, A.A.-G., Cav. Div., Mar. 17th, 1849: *Records of the Scinde Irregular Horse*, 1856, I, 290.

30. Capt. C. A. Delmar, 9th Lancers, to his family, Feb. 1849: *MS. Delmar Letters*, 141–45 (kindly lent to me by their owner, F. M. Delmar, Esq.).

31. [Anon.] *Leaves from the Journal of a Subaltern*, 1849, 147.

32. Malcolm to J. Jacob, Feb. 26th, 1849: *Records of S.I.H.*, 1856, I, 283.

33. Thackwell, E. J., *Narrative of the Second Seikh War*, 1851, 140–45.

34. Marshman, J. C., *Memoirs of Sir H. Havelock*, 1860, 185.

35. Mackenzie, Col. R. H., 'Brig.-Gen. C. R. Cureton, C.B.', *Cavalry Journal*, VII, 1912, 205.

PASSAGES FROM
A LETTER OF PEARMAN TO HIS MOTHER
TRANSCRIBED BY HIM AS AN APPENDIX
TO HIS MEMOIRS

*Upon such letters as these, he probably based
his narrative*

Copy of Letter by me Corpl
Pearman Writen on Battle Feild
Camp Goojrat 24ª February 1849 —
My Dear Mother

      I take up my pen to address
these few lines to you and I hope this
may find you in the injoyment of
good health as thank god This leaves
me at present & I hope all my Brothers
and sister and all the Children are
also in good health. Give my love
to Jane & to Bobs Wife. Ann & to Sollword
& little Frank & kiss all Janeˢ Children
for me. For those was happy days I
spent at home with them. Ann Maria
said she was going to write to me again
but I have never got the letter. I hope
little Louesa is still at Service and
will do well. she was the little thing
that was fond of work when I was
at home. I hope some of the Boys are
able to work by this. And let me know
how my Brothers Williams Children are

are geting on & give my best respects
to Mr & Mrs Hayzell. I hope they are
doing well. & give my best respects to
Joe. Barnham & his Sisters and to
all enquireing freinds

My Dear Mother I will now give you
an Account of the late Campayne as
well as my Memory will alow me to
do. But you will most likely have seen
all about it in the newspapers but
I will give you as true an account
as I Can for the papers dont at all
times Speak the truth. We March from
Umballa last September the 27th of the
Month to form an Army at Lahore. —
which is about 200 Miles South East
of Umballa and after a deal of delay
we reeched Lahore on the 30th of October
and formed an Army of about — 7000 —
Strong & 3 Troops of Guns. 18. in all
The Enemy under the Command of
Rajah Shere Sing was then laying at a
Town Called Wuzzerabad on the Bank

of the river Chenab About 70 miles
north of the City of Lahore. On the
2nd of November we crossed the river.
Ravee north side of the City of Lahore
under the Command of Genl Custin and
on the 5th Novr we had a gallop after
a small portion of the Enemy but
Could not Come up with them I believe
there was one man of the enemy killed
on this occassion. We halted here for
a day or two to allow a Force to Come
to join us under the Command of Genl
Sir Joseph Thackwell. But the Enemy
Moved from their Possion to a Town
much Larger and 30 miles down the
river Chenab our army then took
ground the Westward and halted
About 8 miles from the enemy who
was laying at the Town of Ramnugee.
We were now to wait for reinforcement
which did not join us until the Evening
of the 20th inst. All things now appeared
to be going on very Comfortable and
we was looking forward for a General

the Enemy was in a Nullah and could not be got at. Their Colonel Poor Havelock was killed a good and brave officer 17 men killed and 29 wounded & 30 horses. Genl Barelow went to look were was Havelock and he was shot also & Colnl of the 1st Native Cavelry and several more officers we Burried the Genl & the two Colonels in one Grave. There was little more done this day a little sharp fireing of the Infantry & Artilery. We had one of our Guns got fast in the Serai & we could not get it away it fell into the Enemys hands. our loss was very heavy in fact we got the worst of the day but we held the ground. Night now came on us & Nothing for our horses to eat. After a hard days work and us on their backs for 16 hours. the Night was very cold and lots of our horses got loose and caused a great deal of confusion. We made a fire got a Bullok & killed it —

259 of the river we was laying down on the ground in the hot sun — Most of our men asleep. I was myself we were waiting for orders from Lord Gough. When the Enemy Opened a heavy fire from their artilery upon us & Soon woke us up & Made us jump into our Saddles we soon formed line and got into Battle order when a general Engagement took place about 3 OClock in the Afternoon & by Dark we had well beat them & caused them to retreat to the river Sutlunn — Our loss was but very little in this Battle My regiment lost but one horse. the Enemys loss must have been very great as I saw a Many Dead on the Battle feild next day This was the Battle of Soo-do-lipore — We now Marched to a place called Ailah. and was joined by Lord Gough and the Main Army — We formed a Camp of 20 Thousand of Men and remained here until the

11th January 1849 we were very well
off in this Camp and very Comfortable
and got every thing we wanted & had
plenty of Sports when off Duty when
on Duty it was very hard for Cavelry
so oft to reconnitre the Enemys Camp
on the 11th we Marched at 3 A.m from
this place and on the 13th we Came
to the Main Camp of the Enemy it
was pitched on a hill about 2 miles
from were the Battle was Fought
which was a thick jungle near the
Town of Chillian Walla. About 11. a.m.
we Drove in their advance Parties on
their Main Army and about 2 O'Clock
the Battle raged very hot our Artilery
with that of the Enemys kept up a
Continual roar of Thunder. This was
a very hard fought Battle in the
Midst of a very thick Jungle and
we Could not get at them our fourth
Squadron the Grey Squadron Charged
a Mas of all arms like a Wedge and
our loss was great 25 killed 21 wounded

Also our Capt & Lieut. I was attached
to this Squdron & got a Slight flesh
wound in the arms we did a great
deal of Execution in this Charge
but how we got back none Could tell
H M 24th of foot lost a great number I
think it was 410 men 19 officers and
the Queens Colours of the Regiment
The 15 Sepoys was Cut up and so was
Capt Chestys Troop of horse Artillery
and the Guns taken but we took
12 Guns from the Enemy in the Charge
Our loss altogeather was about 2000
Killed & wounded. The Enemy Loss
was about 5000 Killed & wounded
There was Some Confussion in our
line by the 14th light Dragoon going back
At Night we we retired to a Town or
Large Village in our rear and lay for
the Night the Next morning we
went over the Battle fuild to bury
the dead and get in the wounded
it was a dreadful sight to look
at so many Dead also the horses — —

It began to rain it had a little in the
night. and it Continued to rain for
Several days which made every thing
very uncomfortable We now began to
entrench our Camp as we had to stop
here to wait for the army from
Moultan under the Command of Genl.
Wishe who had just taken Moultan
Our Duty now became very hard. we
Could not take our things off and
ofttimes had to sleep in our arms night
& Day. About the 15 February the Enemy
Shifted their Camp to a Town Called
Goojrat. and on the next day we
moved after them and was there
joined by Genl Wishe army on the 19th
inst when we Saw Some old Camp
Comrades and had a Gloss together
On the 21st inst we had another
Slap at them the Battle Commenced
about 8 Clock A M and by 12 Clock
Noon we had beaten them and put
the whole of their army to Flight
which was followed by part of ours

until they had Crossed the Indus
and on to Pershaw. We took the whole
of their Camp & Carrage & Guns and
Many Thousands Small arms. Our loss
was but small in this Battle and
I hope this will be the last and the
end of the Campayne which I think
it will. About 15 Thousand of our Army
and 60 Guns as gone up the Country
under the Command of Gen'l Gilbert
Who I think will settle things
there — There is a great talk of
Some of the army returning to
quarters very Shortly before the hot
Weather set in I think my Regiment
will return to quarters this Season
this was the Battle of Goojrat —
There as been great riches taken by
the Soldiers at Moultan the 10th foot
& 32 foot & 60 rifles as made a great
deal of Money Some of them Several
hundred Pounds I Shall now
Conclude for the present and I

hope you will answer this
soon as posseable so no more
at present from your affectant
Son

   Corpl John Pearman
  H.M. 3d light Dragoons

P.S Tell my Brother Robert
I got his letter but could not
answer it as it is a great deal
of trouble to get letters sent
away give my best respects to
him and all inquiry freinds

  Direct to
   Corpl John Pearman
  H.M. 3d Light Dragoons
  Army of the Sutledge
    India

INDEX

ALEXANDER, BREVET LT-COL. (LATER GEN. SIR) JAMES, 47, 48, **133**; commands 3rd Tp, 2nd Bde, Bengal Horse Artillery at Aliwal, 40–41, 43
Aliwal, battle of (Jan. 28th, 1846), **41–7**, 104, 131
Artillery:
Bengal Horse, 54
  3rd Tp (European), 2nd Bde, at Aliwal, 40–46, 48, 131
  Capt. Christie's Tp, at Chilianwala, 88–9, 93
Bengal Foot
  'Bengal Tp', 3rd Coy, 4th Bn, 60, 107
British, at Sobraon, 50
horse, history of, 41
Avitabile, Gen., Italian mercenary in Sikh army, 41

BADOWAL, ENGAGEMENT AT (Jan. 21st, 1846), 15, 19, **35–8**, 49
Baker, Sgt.-maj., 3rd L.D., 28, 47; at Badowal, 35–6
Balston, Rev. Dr E., headmaster of Eton, 125, 127, **133**
Bhurtpore, siege of, 1825–6, 39, 45
Bhzee Ram Singh of Jodhpur [?], 58
'Brown Bess' musket, 33, 36
Buckinghamshire Constabulary, Pearman joins, 119; and retires from, 121

CAMBRIDGE, DUKE OF, COMMANDER-IN-CHIEF, 117
Campbell, F.-M. Sir Colin (later Lord Clyde), at Ramnagar, 70
Chilianwala, battle of (Jan. 13th, 1849), 18, **84–93**, 96, 97, 109
cholera, 27, 29

Christie, Capt., at Chilianwala, 88–9, 93; killed, 89
Clarence, Duke of (later William IV), 21
Cureton, Brig.-gen. C.R., 50, **133**; commands cav. at Badowal and Aliwal, 39, 46; at Wazirabad (1848), 69; at Ramnagar, 70–71, 74–5; killed, 75–6

DALHOUSIE, 1ST MARQUESS OF, 88, **133–4**, as Gov.-Gen. (1848), first resists and then grants Gough's demands for troops, 67–8; imposes and then relaxes prohibition on movement upon Gough before Chilianwala, 84; decides to annex Punjab (1849), 105
Dalip Singh, Maharajah, 59
Dick, Maj.-gen. Sir R. H., **134**; commands inf. div. at Sobraon, and killed, 52, 54
Dina Nath, Dewan, 58

ETON COLLEGE, 125, 127; Pearman Police Inspector at, 20, 121, 124

FEROZESHAH, BATTLE OF (Dec. 21st, 1845), 32, 34

GILBERT, LT-GEN. SIR W. R., **134**; commands inf. div. at Sobraon, 53–4
Gough, F.-M. Sir H. (later 1st Visc.), 46, 48, 69, 78, 83, 84, 94, 97, **134–5**; bravery and kindness of, 19; as C-in-C, India, arrives at Mudki (Dec. 1845), 32; detaches Sir H. Smith towards Badowal, 34; at Sobraon, 50; at Lahore peace durbar, 59; forms 'Army of Punjab' (1848), 67–8; at Ramnagar, 71, 74–7; impatience of during action at Sadulapur, 82; at Chilian-

Index